WH… CULT SHOULD I JOIN?

For Maree

Which Cult Should I Join?

A Choose-Your-Own Guidebook for the Spiritually Bereft

Jo Stewart

Smith Street Books

Welcome, spiritually thirsty one.

You've arrived here in search of something – anything – to make this thing called life more meaningful. Like many of us, you've obviously been wondering if there's more to life than the 'eat–sleep–work–Netflix–repeat' cycle. Well, the good news is, there is – there's taxes, debt, divorce and sitting in traffic, too!

If you're searching for belonging, enlightenment and a serious study of cults, you've come to the wrong place. What you will get from this book is understanding. I understand you've had enough. I understand you're fed up. And I understand you're more than a little bit curious about cults. And why the hell not? With mainstream religion having more than a hand in much of the mess we're currently in, it's no wonder many of us are flipping the bird at going to church on Sunday by turning to something else.

It can be hard to ignore the galling hypocrisy that many mainstream religions display without a hint of self-awareness. After accruing thousands of years of compound interest, the Vatican Bank is currently in possession of more than $8 billion in assets and still manages to keep a straight face while sending around the collection plate at the Sunday service. After all, it was rock star-turned-sage Frank Zappa who said, 'The only difference between a cult and a religion is the amount of real estate they own.'

Of course, religion ain't all bad. Religion offers many people salvation, warmth and belonging in a fragile, scary-as-hell world, yet many of us choose to find the same things in our work, our family, our friends, or at the bottom of a bottle of single malt. Then there are the people who turn to cults for answers. Essentially, they're no different from anyone else, they're just searching for somewhere to belong and something to believe in.

So, what constitutes a cult?

Actor Philip Seymour Hoffman once said, 'You can look at anything as a cult. Churches are cults in their own way.' In many ways this book has been written using this logic – when looking at cults, the lines between religion, cult, hate group, secret society and sect are very blurry. In this book, there are no hard and fast rules as to what constitutes a cult (there's already enough dogma in this world).

On your journey to find out which cult best suits you, you'll find everything from cults headed up by egomaniacal nutters prone to magical thinking, to cults with absolutely no one at the wheel. There are highly organised cults worth billions of dollars and shambolic cults without a dime to their name. There are money-making cults disguised as companies and cults that flat out reject consumerism.

To help you out, here are some hints that signal cult-like activity might be going on and tips on how to spot them:

MIND CONTROL AND BRAINWASHING TACTICS

Look for: Are followers subjected to speeches, mantras or propaganda films where attendance is compulsory? Are messages, slogans or beliefs constantly repeated to members?

MONEY SWIMMING MOSTLY UPSTREAM

Look for: Is one person sitting at the top enjoying Cuban cigars and regular baths in Mumm Champagne, while the rest of the community live modestly, sending their income to a leader?

CHARISMATIC, MEGALOMANIACAL LEADER

Look for: Is the leader of the group a charismatic person who proclaims to be 'above' others, either by claiming direct links to God or royalty?

REJECTION OF EVERYTHING OUTSIDE OF THE GROUP

Look for: Is the consumption of media, film or literature outside of what is created by the community banned? Is everything and everyone from 'the outside world' deemed negative or evil?

LACK OF FREE THINKING AND CRITICAL THOUGHT

Look for: Is the questioning of a leader's ideas or motives discouraged or punished? Is healthy debate disallowed?

ISOLATION FROM FAMILY MEMBERS AND FRIENDS

Look for: Are members ostracised or completely cut off from family members, friends and community members not within the group?

UNBELIEVABLE CLAIMS

Look for: Is someone claiming to have a direct line of communication with God? Are they suggesting they are the second coming themselves? Asking you to sign over all your property and wealth to them for 'safekeeping' during the apocalypse? Essentially, if your bullshit detector is going off when a 'guru' is speaking, then you're probably in a cult!

To begin your journey down the yellow brick road, we'll start with a really simple question.

Do you believe that Jesus Christ was the Son of God and once walked the earth?

Yes. → Turn to page 46

No. → Turn to page 24

Not sure yet. → Turn to page 30

You're now a member of ...

The Magnificat Meal Movement

Get ready to part with large sums of cash, you've just joined an obscure Australian cult responsible for fleecing the pockets of unsuspecting followers. As a part of the Magnificat Meal Movement, you'll fall under the spell of a self-styled religious guru with a penchant for travelling first class and driving Mercedes Benz cars. Once you cotton on to the manipulative tactics used to drain funds from your accounts, you'll be banished from the cult but you will soon regain a sense of self and a whole new lease of life, as many brave ex-followers have. You'll also regain a discretionary income, as you won't be throwing cash at a certain someone's next luxury car or first-class holiday to Spain …
all inthe name of God, of course.

While this cult may sound like a weight-loss program, the only thing members of the Magnificat Meal Movement are losing in large amounts is money. Slipping onto Australia's national radar in the 1990s, this cult was co-founded by a woman called Debra Geileskey (known by her followers as Mother Debramarie Burslem). Operating from the small town of Helidon in Queensland's Lockyer Valley, the Magnificat Meal Movement has Catholic roots, with visions of Virgin Mary and direct contact with Jesus figuring in Burslem's sales pitch to potential followers.

Following a familiar script, followers gave up their properties and money in exchange for a life lived as Slaves of the Eucharist, with the charismatic sect leader reportedly raking in more than $20 million from members. Because no cult leader is complete without a list of outlandish claims, it's been reported that Mother Debramarie Burslem claimed to be the rightful heir to the British throne and to have received direct messages from the Virgin Mary.

When disgruntled members started to realise they were being scammed, the heat was turned right up on Burslem. With the media knocking on her door and the authorities closing in, Burslem 'retired' (read: fled) to Vanuatu where she now lives in exile in a million-dollar property protected by high walls topped with cut glass – the preferred palace of most garden-variety con artists and charlatans who like to invoke the name of God to swindle trusting people out of their hard-earned dough.

One major factor when considering your cult options is location, because everyone has a different idea of paradise.

One person's heaven may be another person's hell, and, with so many cults choosing to hide away from the world in compounds, it's a really good idea to choose wisely just in case your vision of utopia does not include living in an underground bunker on a ranch in Shitsville, USA.

If you had to live in one environment for the rest of your life, which would you prefer?

A tropical island. → Turn to page 56 to keep searching

A quietly creepy desert. → Find your cult on page 116

A big, thriving, urban metropolis. → Find your cult on page 120

Deliverance country, USA. → Find your cult on page 134

You're now a member of ...

The Unarius Academy of Science

Don your favourite golden lamé cape, tease your hair up high and strap yourself in for a wild ride, you've just joined the Unarius Academy of Science. Reeking of the 1980s, this flamboyant yet harmless Californian cult fuses a love of UFOs with a gift for performance art to create a fantastical cult perfect for lovers of sci-fi, community theatre and fancy-dress parties. As a member of the Unarius Academy of Science, you'll be part of a cult that believes a whole lot of utterly mind-boggling stuff, including that the 'Asian race' comes from Mars and that our alien brothers and sisters will arrive on a spaceship super-fleet to turn our deserts into vegetable gardens. You'll also contribute to some of the zaniest, low-budget movies ever shown on public access TV. While many cults like to hide their activities behind closed compound doors, this is one cult that is unafraid of the limelight. Step forward for your close-up.

Founded in 1954, the Unarius (UNiversal ARticulate Interdimensional Understanding of Science) Academy of Science, was brought to life in Los Angeles, California by a married couple called Ernest and Ruth Norman. With Ernest controlling the organisation from 1954 until his death in 1972 and Ruth taking over from 1972 until her death in 1993, this cult has two distinct dynasties with very different flavours.

Ernest was a self-proclaimed psychic and prolific author who wrote books by 'channelling' messages from the cosmos. With Ernest claiming to be the reincarnation of Jesus (among many others), both he and Ruth were big believers in past-life therapy and incorporated it into their teachings.

While this cult ticked along quite nicely from the 1950s to the 1970s, it really reached its zenith in the 1980s, largely thanks to Ruth (now going by the name Uriel) and her love of creating out-of-this-world movies. Beamed across America on public access TV during the 80s and 90s, the Unarius films are mind-bending, interstellar journeys into another dimension (a dimension where purple and gold crushed velvet capes are the standard uniform and special effects are not special but to be applied liberally in every film scene).

Unsurprisingly, Uriel was also into predicting the future, forecasting that aliens would arrive on planet Earth in 2001. When the aliens failed to show up as predicted (when will cult leaders learn that it's not wise to give firm timelines for doomsday prophesies?) many members lost faith and left the cult. Despite this, the Unarius Academy of Science still operates from its head office in El Cajon, California, even lending Uriel's beyond kitsch flying saucer-themed Cadillac to the local community for special events.

More recently, Uriel's magical movie back-catalogue has gained a cult following with the cool kids, drawn in by the 80s UFO aesthetic and killer synth soundtracks. With movie screenings in hip hotels in West Hollywood, could the Unarius Academy of Science be on the cult comeback trail? Let's hope so!

You're now a member of ...

The Remnant Fellowship

Be prepared to shed some pounds – you've just joined a controversial cult where people turn to God to help them lose weight. As a member of the Remnant Fellowship, you'll pray away your Burger King cravings by asking for divine intervention in your quest to be thin. While some of us turn to Weight Watchers, others to the gym or the doctor's office, you have chosen God and the sanctimonious fat-shaming crew from the Remnant Fellowship Church to pray the pounds away.

Based in Tennessee (but with branches all over America) the Remnant Fellowship is headed up by former dietician Gwen Shamblin. By equating overeating with sinning, the founders of the Remnant Fellowship have been able to shame thousands of followers into new-found thinness with their customised Christian weight-loss program called the Weigh Down Workshop.

So what makes the Remnant Fellowship a cult and not just a harmless Christian group with members who are keen on staying trim? The Remnant Fellowship displays classic hallmarks of cult-like activity including encouraging members to isolate themselves from friends and family who aren't also part of the Remnant Fellowship and to avoid any reading materials that haven't come from the Fellowship. This group also takes a hard-line approach to the discipline and control of children, reportedly encouraging parents to hit their children with objects. And of course, there's the obvious wealth drifting upward to the founder of the church, a propensity to take detractors to court and a string of ex-members publicly warning others to steer clear.

And as if advocating child abuse in the name of God isn't a big enough red flag, the founder of this cult once used the Holocaust to sell her program, citing Nazi concentration camps as a good example of how people can survive by eating less. Okayyyy then...

While encouraging healthy eating habits is no doubt a good thing in a country that posts record levels of obesity and other illnesses caused by poor eating habits, there's something distinctly unpalatable about invoking the name of God in order to sell a weight-loss program to desperate people keen to fit into their bikinis next summer. Essentially, the Remnant Fellowship is a cult dedicated to warding off the evil urge to eat tasty things and making supreme amounts of money from selling weight-loss programs and books, while allowing followers to have absolutely zero fun in the process.

The world's most notorious cults are probably those that have generated headlines due to their penchant for violence, leading to their inevitable grisly ends.

From epic shootouts to mass suicide pacts, cult leaders may be good at harping on about oneness and peace, but boy, are they even better at taking up arms to murder people.

With that in mind, where do you stand on the ownership of weapons?

I believe that it's everyone's right to amass as much weaponry as they like. How else are we supposed to protect ourselves from intruders or foreign invaders?

Find your cult on page 22

I really have no need to own guns or weapons. We are here to love, not kill each other.

Find your cult on page 26

I don't have much of a stance on weaponry. However, it's about time the government took a look at relaxing restrictive polygamy laws.

Find your cult on page 28

You're now a member of ...

Buddhafield

As a member of the Buddhafield community, you'll follow a strange-yet-charismatic leader who seems to have all the answers, but is actually just one big walking riddle himself. Drawn to the concept of giving and receiving universal love, you'll most likely join the Buddhafield community as a fast-track to spiritual awakening. Yet mixed in with the bliss of living with like-minded believers into everything from hypnosis to communicating with astral beings living on other planes, there's a sinister underbelly to this seemingly free-spirited community. In Buddhafield, follow your bliss at your own risk.

Started in Los Angeles in the 1980s by a former porn actor with a persecution complex, Buddhafield was marketed as a spiritual community for people seeking peace and enlightenment. Unsurprisingly, people were interested in this utopian fantasy and soon more than a hundred people were living together in harmony under the Buddhafield banner.

Buddhafield's 'guru' was a South American man who went by quite a few different names, including Michel, Andreas and 'the Teacher'. A practising hypnotherapist with a penchant for wearing nothing but a pair of Speedos and sunglasses (creep alert), 'the Teacher' banned followers from having sex with each other, yet often forced them to have sex with him during his specially patented 'cleansing' sessions.

In retrospect, everything about Buddhafield screams 'cult'. There's the shady, hypocritical leader at the top; the operating locations of the Hollywood Hills and South Austin (both prime locations for cult activity); and, of course, there's the obligatory documentary called *Holy Hell* that debuted at the Sundance Film Festival, made by an ex-follower out to expose the cult leader. No doubt about it, Buddhafield ticks all the cult boxes.

Despite operating for more than twenty years, Buddhafield pretty much imploded when followers started to call out the leader's hypocritical bullshit and began taking the brave steps towards building a new life, sans-cult. Proving that old habits die hard, 'Michel' has reportedly changed his name to Reyji and has started a new cult in Hawaii.

You're now a member of ...

The Branch Davidians

Howdy partner, you've just joined a cult that is more Texas than Texas itself. As a member of the Branch Davidians, you'll follow a Houston native called David Koresh. With a penchant for stockpiling high-powered firearms and military-grade weaponry, punishing children with beatings and taking on 'wives' as young as eleven, living under the rule of Koresh isn't fun for anyone. As a Branch Davidian you have to comply to very strict rules that govern everything from what food is allowed on your plate to how you will die. Unless you're one of the lucky ones who manages to escape, you'll end up dying alongside your cult leader in a Texas-style firefight that shocks the world.

Founded in the 1930s, the Branch Davidians operated like any other Christian religious sect for decades, until a fellow named David Koresh joined in the 1980s and set the cat among the pigeons. Koresh gained followers within the Branch Davidian group by claiming the gift of prophecy, challenging the anointed prophet of the sect, George Roden. Like two bulls locking horns, Roden and Koresh went at it for a while – Roden even exhumed a human corpse from a cemetery and challenged Koresh to raise the dead by bringing it back to life. After a while, a splinter group of Davidians formed in support of Koresh and started a new branch of the Branch Davidians (they should have been known as Branch Branch Davidians).

The breakaway group preferred to be called 'Koreshians' and, after setting up shop in a compound on a sprawling rural property near Waco, Texas, they lived under Koresh's bizarre rule. And bizarre it truly was, with Koresh sparing no cost when investing in high-powered assault rifles and ammunition, while totally forgetting to provide funds for basics like running water, sanitation and heating.

Koresh's rule follows a very familiar narrative common to many male cult leaders with a God complex. He took many wives, reportedly raped children as young as eleven and beat up kids for behaviour as inconsequential as spilling a drink. He forced all the men in the group to be celibate (except himself, of course). He also raved about the impending end of the world and the holy battle that was soon to take place. There are so many red flags waving here, it's hard to know where to start.

Brainwashing his followers into believing the outside world was a very dangerous place (uh huh), hundreds of his followers were either too scared or too taken in by him to leave the abusive squalor they lived in. Despite this, the external tide began to turn against Koresh when the authorities became concerned by the obvious signs of child abuse and the stockpiling of illegal weaponry within the compound.

By 1993, Koresh realised his kingdom was crumbling and after the Bureau of Alcohol, Tobacco, Firearms and Explosives (ATF) tried to issue a search warrant, all hell broke loose. While the details have been disputed, what is known is that shots were fired, agents were killed, and a terrifying 51-day siege began.

Playing out on television screens all over the world, the siege ended when the FBI got involved. After attempting to force Koresh to surrender by using a combination of sleep-deprivation tactics (like playing loud music and recordings of jet plane noise) and negotiation techniques, the FBI raided the property. After an intense firefight, three separate fires broke out on the property, allegedly all started by Koresh. By the end of the siege more than 80 people had been killed with most dying from gunshot wounds, burns and smoke inhalation. Many of the victims were children. David Koresh was counted among the dead.

So, you don't believe in God.

This is great news for you, you dirty little heathen. Now we can pretty much skip past all of the cults that are basically warped offshoots of Christianity to focus on the really interesting cults that take cues from much more radical places than mainstream religion. My friend, things are about to get very interesting for you.

Do you believe that alien life forms exist?

Yes. I believe it's possible that aliens are out there.

Turn to page 100 to keep searching

Nope. I think that we're the sole occupants of the entire solar system and my belief in aliens only extends to watching episodes of 80s sitcom *Alf*.

Turn to page 36 to keep searching

You're now a member of ...

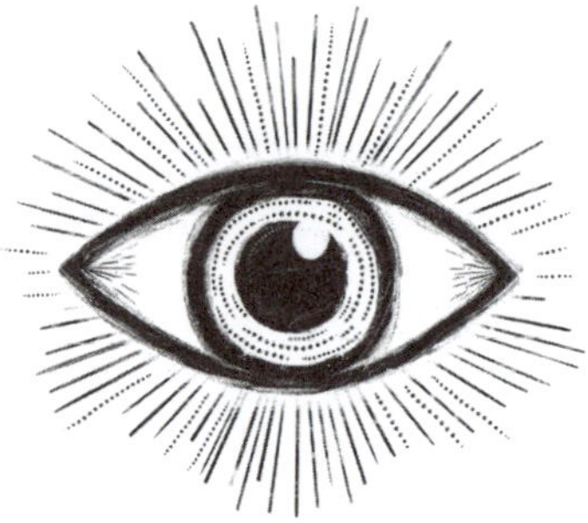

The Hare Krishnas

Sing it! 'Hare Krishna, Hare Krishna, Krishna, Krishna, Hare, Hare, Hare Rama, Hare Rama, Rama, Rama, Hare, Hare.' Put on your saffron robes, embrace celibacy and get ready to bang your drum and jingle your bells, you're now a Hare Krishna. Your days in this neo-Hindu cult will be spent meditating, singing, dancing and volunteering in kitchens making vegetarian curries for the Hare Krishna food program. Lucky you'll be so busy with all that singing, dancing and cooking that you probably won't have time to mind that you're forbidden from having sex for pleasure, smoking, taking drugs and drinking alcohol, coffee and tea. Oh, and you can't eat meat either. And cancel that trip to Vegas, gambling is also forbidden. Oh dear ... What. Have. You. Done?

Founded in New York in the mid 1960s, the International Society for Krishna Consciousness (ISKCON) was the brainchild of Srila Prabhupada, who saw an opening in the religious movement category and really went for it.

Appealing to westerners who wanted to take a dip into Eastern mysticism in the heady days of the 60s, the Hare Krishna movement believes that out of all the millions of Hindu gods out there, Krishna is the one to put your money on. Following a strict no meat, no coffee, no tea, no alcohol, no gambling, no sex-for-pleasure, no fun regime, the Hare Krishna's get their kicks from chanting and dancing in urban locations. And who hasn't at one time secretly wanted to join that Hare Krishna conga line while on a night out on the turps?

While appearing to be super friendly and fun loving, some seriously dodgy attitudes towards women and gay people have seen this cult land itself in hot water. Hare Krishna women are expected to adopt a submissive attitude towards men, something that doesn't tend to go down well with most women these days. Gay people are also given a bit of a hard time in the scriptures, but with Boy George reportedly dabbling in Hare Krishna life, it's unclear if this claim is indeed true.

Despite attracting a fair bit of scorn, the Hare Krishna movement continues to grow in popularity and gets more and more organised each year. With Hare Krishna enterprises popping up all over the globe, people can dine at Hare Krishna vegetarian restaurants, stretch it out at Hare Krishna yoga centres, escape the city at Hare Krishna retreat centres and read up on Krishna consciousness with a subscription to the thrilling Hare Krishna *Back to Godhead* magazine.

While it's easy to be cynical towards an organisation that requires its members to sing and dance outside bars at night, the Hare Krishnas have also established the world's largest vegetarian food relief program. Feeding millions of needy people through their Food for Life program, the Hare Krishnas run a global network of kitchens, cafés and mobile food vans dedicated to ensuring people experiencing poverty and homelessness can receive a meal.

No doubt there's some seriously cultish behaviour going on here – strict rules of engagement, matching uniforms, oppression of women and potential brainwashing via mantras, but, on the flipside, these guys are also feeding the homeless and bringing low-cost yoga classes to a city near you!

You're now a member of ...

The Fundamentalist Church of Jesus Christ of Latter-Day Saints (FLDS)

Even though this cult's motto is 'keep sweet', there's no way to sugar-coat this: you've just joined one of the biggest, baddest, boldest cults currently operating in the USA. As a member of the Fundamentalist Church of Jesus Christ of Latter-Day Saints, you'll live a highly controlled and ordered life without things like television, newspapers, dogs (!?), tattoos, the internet, toys and birthdays – all of which were outlawed by the (currently incarcerated) spiritual leader / head child-molester of the church, Warren Jeffs.

As a member of FLDS, you'll spend your time praying for the release of Warren Jeffs, because he's handed over the responsibility of his release to his people, who apparently just aren't praying hard enough. Or perhaps you'll be one of the lucky ones who makes a successful escape and ends up writing a best-selling, tell-all book. In that case, you'll spend your days doing the American talk show circuit, basking in the glory of publicly calling bullshit on what is considered one of the largest cases of systematic child abuse on the planet. Go you!

A radical offshoot of Mormonism, the Fundamentalist Church of Jesus Christ of Latter-Day Saints (FLDS) is one hell of a controversy magnet, mainly due to its belief in practising polygamy and 'marrying' off girls as young as twelve to men as old as sixty.

With up to 10,000 members worshipping at churches in Texas, South Dakota, North Dakota, Colorado, British Columbia in Canada, and many other areas in North America, FLDS is largely associated with the state of Utah. The history of FLDS is a long and pretty boring account of delusional middle-aged white men fighting for leadership and control of the church, all while committing sex crimes against children.

Life in FLDS is very controlled, with bans on everything from fishing to rock music. Women are forced to wear floor-length, pastel-coloured prairie dresses and are forbidden such trifles as wearing make-up, cutting their hair, getting piercings or choosing their own husband. In fact, they don't even get to choose who they have sex with, as only sanctioned male members of the community are allowed to impregnate (read: rape) women of FLDS. Of course, homosexuality is forbidden, as is interracial marriage, and you can forget about going to an outside high school or university. It's home-schooling in a FLDS-run school (where you'll learn amazing things such as that the moon landing never happened and the leader of FLDS is actually the President of the United States), or nothing. A few things that aren't banned though (at least for leaders) are paedophilia, rape and the use of child labour on farms.

The most recent prophet, Warren Jeffs, has really outdone himself, ending up on the FBI's 'Most Wanted' list in 2006. Following his capture and arrest, the leader of the church (and husband to almost 80 women) became a convicted felon. Despite being incarcerated, serving a life sentence (and then some) for committing child sex offences, he is still accepted as the spiritual leader of FLDS.

With Jeffs imprisoned, the day-to-day management of FLDS has fallen to his brothers, Lyle and Seth. Both are now being investigated by the authorities for reportedly masterminding a food stamp fraud scheme. If convicted, they too will likely serve jail time, along with many other members of FLDS. Following the capture and incarceration of Warren Jeffs, other FLDS properties were raided in an attempt to stop the rampant paedophilia occurring within church walls. Many more male leaders were arrested and charged with sex crimes against children, including Raymond Merrill Jessop and Merrill Leroy Jessop, both spiritual figureheads of the FLDS in Texas.

So is FLDS a church that has a right to worship whatever it wants or is it nothing more than an organised paedophile ring run by racist, woman-hating criminals? You decide.

Hollywood movies, cult leaders, late-night television evangelical preachers and sometimes even politicians are obsessed with the idea of the end of the world.

Doomsday, the apocalypse, end of days – whatever you want to call it, for generations, hordes of people have predicted that our planet is going to hell in a handbasket. Yet for some reason it just keeps on spinning.

So, do you believe that the world will end in your lifetime?

Absolutely. I know it for a fact. → Turn to page 80 to keep searching

I'm not sure. But I am open to the idea. → Turn to page 124 to keep searching

You're now a member of ...

The Cult of Amma

Holy hell, you've just joined a cult led by a woman who is simultaneously loved and hated by many. As a disciple of 'Amma the Hugging Saint', you'll follow a middle-aged Indian woman across the world as she hugs her way around the planet. Bringing peace, love and healing to anyone who can be bothered lining up for nine hours for a hug, Amma is both a Hindu phenomenon and a force to be reckoned with. She is both admired and despised. Your experience with this cult will largely depend on what side of the Amma fence you sit on.

Amma (meaning 'mother') is a complex human riddle that may never be solved. Even film maker Louis Theroux had a go at unravelling the cult of Amma and came up empty-handed (but he seemed to have a good time in the process). Considered to be a spiritual guru and bona fide religious leader in her homeland, Amma has made a name for herself as a globetrotting super hugger. Bringing new meaning to the term 'stage five clinger', Amma simply hugs the shit out of everyone she can get her hands on. Forget the twee 'free hugs' movement – Amma started that caper long before a random dude started standing on busy city streets offering no-strings-attached cuddles.

Attending an Amma the Hugging Saint event is a bizarre experience that tends to leave most people dazed and confused. The whole experience is a bit of a circus – attendees are required to sit on the floor and wait for hours, then crawl up to Amma on hands and knees when their number is finally called, lottery-style. With more merch stands than Glastonbury Festival, Amma peddles all manner of spiritual souvenirs, including flower garlands, prayer books and stuffed toys. So, while the hugs are free, attendees will still usually end up parting with cash (either at the merch stands or via the donation bucket). When you consider that Amma has claimed to have hugged millions of people, the amount of money flowing into her coffers must be exceptional.

So, what's not to love about a woman who has dedicated her life to bringing healing hugs to the world? I mean, everyone needs to hug it out once in a while, and Amma's simply providing comfort to people in need of some platonic loving, right? Well, the problem with Amma has been addressed in several unflattering books, blogs and articles claiming to expose the malevolent truth behind her tender-hearted exterior. Detractors allege that Amma has engaged in abusive conduct towards her staff, hidden millions of dollars in foreign bank accounts and excommunicated anyone who dared to question her authority. It's hard to tell where the truth lies, but either way, anyone who claims to be a 'guru' is a bit on the nose, and crawling on the floor to receive a hug from someone sitting on an elevated platform is pretty cultish. The jury might be out on the claims against Amma, but our cult detectors are registering a direct hit.

You're now a member of ...

Fiat Lux

As a member of Fiat Lux ('let there be light' in Latin) you'll live a semi-monastic life in a small town located within the Black Forest in Germany. Apart from swanning around with other followers in matching robes, you'll spend most of your time waiting for the apocalypse to come to town. Of course, the apocalypse will come in alien form, because what is a doomsday cult without a sprinkling of extraterrestrials?

Led by a Swiss woman called Erika Bertschinger (also known as Uriella), Fiat Lux merges apocalypticism with UFOs to create a good old-fashioned doomsday cult. Following a familiar format, Uriella claims to receive direct messages from God and the Virgin Mary, and like many other cult leaders she has also predicted the end of the world on numerous occasions, except her version of Armageddon comes with a twist. According to followers of Fiat Lux, the world as we know it will indeed end, but for the enlightened, benevolent alien-folk will arrive on flying saucers to sweep them up off to safety on another planet. Of course, this expensive transport doesn't come for free, and followers need to hand over their life savings in order to hitch a ride to infinity and beyond.

After the world failed to end as predicted in 1998, Uriella merely explained away this failed prediction by saying she prayed the apocalypse away to another day (nice save!). While being able to postpone an apocalypse is a fine talent, Uriella also has many other talents to share with the world, including scamming her followers out of millions of dollars and selling false treatments through her homeopathy business. Let there be light, indeed ...

So, no God and no aliens either?

Okay, I can see you're in the market for a very special type of cult. You are not seeking salvation from above, so clearly you are searching for something on a more terrestrial (or even subterranean) level.

Sometimes, we should stop overthinking things and let our senses lead the way. By allowing our senses to take over, we're able to tap into another side of ourselves to access intuitive knowledge (the type of knowledge that could lead to discovering your perfect cult).

With this in mind, follow your nose to spiritual satisfaction by answering the following question.

Do you secretly enjoy the smell of sulphur?

Yes. I often find myself hanging out near thermal geysers and bubbling mud pools, getting high off the sulphur fumes that send everyone else running. It's my secret shame.

Find your cult on page 102

No. Gross.

Turn to page 74 to keep searching

You're now a member of ...

Church Universal and Triumphant (CUT)

Start stockpiling toilet paper, semi-automatic weapons and other essentials, you've just joined an American doomsday cult responsible for creating one of the most avant-garde recordings in music history. As a member of Church Universal and Triumphant (CUT), you'll follow aptly named leader Elizabeth Clare Prophet, whose talents include talking to dead people and inaccurately predicting the apocalypse. You'll also make recording history by contributing to one of the strangest records ever released, a highly sought-after recording of frenetic, otherworldly chanting that has been sampled by DJs wide and far.

Church Universal and Triumphant was formed as an offshoot of another cult called The Summit Lighthouse, started by an American man named Mark L. Prophet in 1958. Following Prophet's passing in 1973, the organisation was placed in the hands of his wife, Elizabeth, who soon incorporated her own little spiritual project, Church Universal and Triumphant.

Claiming to communicate with a collection of ascended masters including everyone from Buddha to Confucius and Saint Germain (the Christian saint, not the 90s acid jazz musician), Elizabeth Prophet grew Church Universal Triumphant rapidly. Moving the spiritual headquarters from California to Montana in the 1980s, follower numbers swelled to thousands, if not hundreds of thousands.

Playing on thoroughly contemporary fears around impending nuclear war, people were drawn to the church's mystical take on spirituality that incorporated Christian, Taoist and Buddhist teachings, along with a side serve of esotericism. With Elizabeth Clare Prophet possessing a great sense of showmanship and a talent for hypnotic chanting at high speed, it's no wonder people were taken in by this lady with a direct line to the gods.

Following the prophetic announcement that the world was soon to end, the group went all *Doomsday Preppers*, building an underground bunker system and amassing food, weapons and other all-American essentials. As is so often the case with doomsday cults, when the world didn't end, followers kind of woke up to the scam and dropped off the scene. After falling ill, Elizabeth Clare Prophet stepped down as leader in 1999, then passed away ten years later.

Church Universal and Triumphant was largely forgotten by society until it popped up on the pop culture radar following the mysterious release of an album called *Sounds of American Doomsday Cults: Volume 14*. Consisting of loops of freaky-as chanting and spoken word rants performed by Elizabeth Prophet and her followers, the album produced more questions than answers. Who released this? Where are Volumes 1–13? The bizarre nature of the recording resulted in a cult following of another kind, with the original gaining fans in the avante garde music scene and various musicians and DJs, including Fatboy Slim, sampling the work.

Despite declining membership numbers, Church Universal and Triumphant still exists today. It's doubtful it will ever reach the heights of the heady 80s and 90s, but thanks to the unearthing of the obscure recording made by the group decades ago, the Church Universal and Triumphant is enjoying a moment in the sun once again.

When it comes to the rights of women, cults typically have just as much trouble with equality as mainstream religions do.

Which really doesn't bode well since it's a pretty basic concept to grasp. Despite this, some cults have really gotten with the program in a big way and alien-worship cults are often at the forefront of equal rights for all citizens of the universe.

Do you believe that women should have the right to be topless in public?

Hell yeah! Free the nipple all the way. → Find your cult on page 126

Not sure about women but I'd totally follow a shirtless man. → Find your cult on page 20

No. Both women and men should keep their shirts on when in public. → Turn to page 30 to keep searching

You're now a member of ...

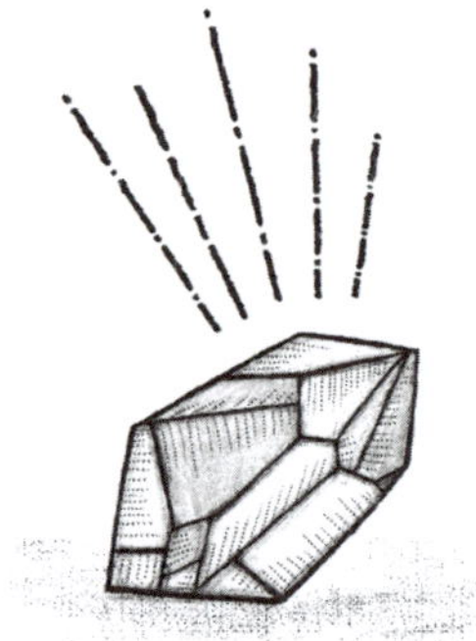

The Orange People

Hopefully, lurid burnt orange is your colour, because you've just joined a cult headed up by a leader with a thirst for the good things in life, namely: sex, luxury vehicles, bioterrorism and orange clothing. As a member of the Orange People, you'll walk away from what Western mainstream religions have to offer and embrace the allure of Eastern mysticism. You'll don orange robes, get involved in 70s-style sex-fests with other followers and possibly be part of a rampantly stupid attempt to rig a local election. Life as a member of the Orange People is one hell of a wild ride, while it lasts.

Led by a charismatic Indian man referred to as Bhagwan Shree Rajneesh (more widely known as Osho later in life), the Orange People, also known as the Rajneesh movement, rose to fame in the 1970s and 80s, before vanishing into obscurity after a major scandal scattered the cult members to the wind.

With Eastern mysticism growing in popularity in the 70s (thanks, George Harrison), many westerners became hooked on the idea of giving up their possessions, quitting their jobs and living in communes ruled by 'free love'. And free love is exactly what they got. With ashram life reportedly one big partner-swapping orgy session after another, it wasn't hard for the Orange People to gain new followers.

Communes sprung up everywhere from Australia to the USA, but it was one particular state in America that caught Bhagwan Shree Rajneesh's eye. With donations from followers around the world, he built a spiritual mini-city in a small town in Oregon. However, locals soon became annoyed at the Orange People moving in on their territory and tensions rose between local residents and the thousands of orange-robed followers who had flocked to this sleepy corner of the Pacific Northwest to follow a man who used his 93-strong fleet of Rolls Royces to perform 'drive-by blessings'.

Things came to a head in a most explosive manner when some of the Orange People took matters into their own hands. In an attempt to rig the results of local elections, a group of followers committed the first and largest bioterrorism attack on American soil by releasing salmonella into the buffets and salad bars of local restaurants. Although more than 700 people fell ill with salmonella poisoning, no one died, and the attack goes down in history as one of the most bizarre attempts to rig an election. Taking voters out with a bout of diarrhoea is about as low as politics can go.

Following the 'salad bar incident' the key perpetrators of the crime were arrested and charged, and Bhagwan Shree Rajneesh effectively ended the existence of the Orange People. Encouraging followers to stop wearing orange, Bhagwan Shree Rajneesh left Oregon and reinvented himself as Osho. Ever the showman, Osho went on to publish a range of best-selling books (that still sell in their millions) and set up a luxury retreat centre in India that still exists today.

Despite dying in India in 1990, Osho is a genuine social media superstar and the darling of people who like to post inane inspirational quotes on Instagram. With more than 125,000 followers on the official Osho Twitter account and a series of popular YouTube videos, Osho's popularity endures despite his involvement in a bioterrorist attack and wide-scale visa fraud. Oh, and then there's his well-known rampant homophobia and sickening belief that deaf and blind children should be euthanised. Osho may not have been the full quid, but as a cult leader he was 100% pure Teflon.

You're now a member of ...

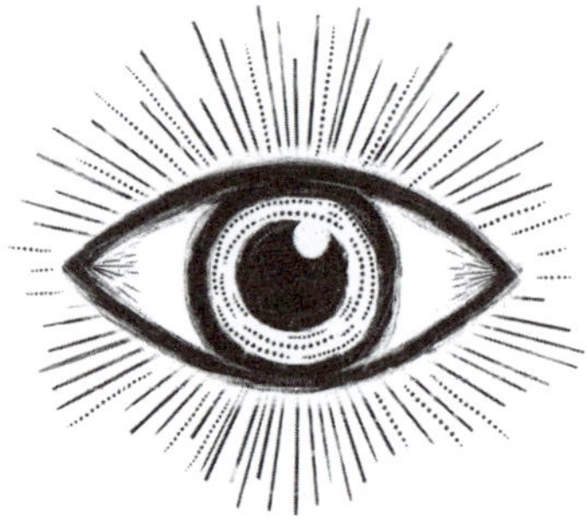

The Brotherhood of the Golden Arrow

Well, well, well, you old horn bag – you've just joined one of the raunchiest cults in history. Living in Paris in the 1930s, you'll be drawn into the world of sex magic (yes ... sex magic) by a Russian woman named Maria de Naglowska who also dabbled in Satanism in her spare time. As a member of the Brotherhood of the Golden Arrow, you'll be awakened to the transformative power of sex (Amen!) alongside avant-garde artists and literary types operating in the Parisian arts scene at the time. While short-lived, your time in this cult is certainly memorable.

The brainchild of Russian occultist, mystic and Satanist Maria de Naglowska, the Brotherhood of the Golden Arrow operated for a few hot and heavy years in Paris in the early 1930s. An early proponent of autoerotic strangulation, Maria developed a following among open-minded Parisian artists, writers and creative types, including Man Ray and Andre Breton, and eventually made her High Priestess status official with the birth of the Brotherhood of the Golden Arrow.

A well-travelled broad with an eye for the surreal and a penchant for hosting elaborate ceremonies, Maria de Naglowska effectively tapped into a market of people keen on things such as nudity, over-the-top banquets and satanic sex rituals. As a down-on-her-luck single mother, you have to hand it to Maria for finding a way to make money and have fun at the same time.

After a few rollicking years, things came to a crashing halt after Maria experienced an unfortunate vision. Foreseeing her own death, Maria retreated to Switzerland where she passed away a year later in 1936. Her legacy endures today with her controversial books on sex magic still available for sale on Amazon.

Ah, so you believe in Jesus. Great start.

Many cults begin as an offshoot of a mainstream religion. This not only makes it easier for cult leaders to find followers (because they can simply poach them from other churches) it also gives their claims some validity as many people are generally comfortable with the idea of Jesus, Mary and Joseph.

As the Christianity handbook, the Bible is full of ideas that may have seemed like a good idea thousands of years ago, but just don't translate into modern society.

Do you believe that the world would be a better place if everyone followed the Ten Commandments?

Yes. This would be most pleasant. I'm in. → Find your cult on page 50

Um ... I think the Ten Commandments offer good boundaries but it's just not possible for sinning humans to follow every commandment. → Find your cult on page 54

Hell, no! → Turn to page 52 to keep searching

You're now a member of ...

The Family International (TFI)

You've just joined a cult where free love meets fundamentalism. You might not believe that those two things can coexist but the Family International proved everyone wrong (and hurt an incredible amount of followers in the process). As a member of TFI, you'll be involved in many highly questionable sex rituals (some of which are probably illegal, too) in the name of Christ. You'll follow the word of a reclusive man with some truly mind-blowingly bad ideas on how to 'get closer to God'. With a dash of apocalypticism and more than a smidgen of hypocrisy, TFI is just not OK.

Going through more name changes than The Artist Formerly Known as Prince (may he rest in peace), The Family International has also operated under the names Teens for Christ, the Children of God, The Family, and the Family of Love.

Founded by a reclusive anti-Semite called David 'Moses' Berg, TFI sprung up on the sect scene in southern California in the 1960s. Unlike many charismatic cult leaders, Berg didn't live among his followers, instead communicating his teachings via letters (his varied beliefs included predictions that Comet Kohoutek signified the end of days and that the Antichrist would soon rise to rule the world). Fearing possible assassination and legal troubles, all letters were written in isolation and disseminated to followers in hundreds of communes throughout the world.

Spanning several dynasties, resurrections and reincarnations, controversy seems to plague the Family International, and not without good reason. Responsible for some of the most deranged spiritual practices going around, The Family International have been accused of everything from child abuse to running organised prostitution rings masquerading as spiritual worship.

During the 70s, the group were responsible for coining the phrase 'Flirty Fishing', which described the practice of sending female followers out to have sexual intercourse with men in order to persuade them to join the cult. The Family essentially turned female followers into sex workers – all in the name of God. Due to fears around the advent of AIDS (birth control and any form of protection or contraception were banned by TFI), 'Flirty Fishing' was abandoned in the 80s.

If that's not bizarre enough, followers were also encouraged to imagine Jesus was with them while they were masturbating or having sex. Because homosexuality was forbidden, male followers were encouraged to imagine that Jesus was a woman in order to avoid a spiritual conflict. While it's unknown how popular this practice was, it's pretty safe to assume that getting jiggy with Jesus is a bit of a boner killer.

Even though Berg passed away in the mid-90s, the group still exists today, albeit in a very watered down form. As with many cults, when the founder or figurehead dies, the cult either reinvents itself or dies off. In the case of TFI, several name changes weren't really enough to cast off the stench of sexual exploitation and child abuse that emanates from the group, and, as result, numbers today are reportedly nowhere near what they were in the 60s, 70s and 80s.

These days, TFI is still the subject of much discussion, with former cult members, including celebrities Rose McGowan and Joaquin Phoenix, choosing to speak to the media about the trauma of growing up in TFI. While Berg may have died decades ago, his influence continues to send shockwaves through the lives of any who are unlucky enough to encounter his dangerous doctrines.

You're now a member of ...

The Movement for the Restoration of the Ten Commandments of God

You have chosen… poorly. Very, very poorly. You've just joined a doomsday cult responsible for one of the biggest mass murders this planet has ever seen. As a member of Uganda's Movement for the Restoration of the Ten Commandments of God, you'll hand your life (and property and savings) over to five low-rent criminals with the gift of the gab and a callous disregard for human life. Believing that the world is going to end in the year 2000 (didn't we all?), you entrust your soul to the leaders of the Movement who, true to their politician roots, are big on promises but crummy on delivery. Trigger warning: involvement in this deplorable cult doesn't bode well for anyone.

The Movement for the Restoration of the Ten Commandments of God is what happens when a moonshine brewer and a bottom-feeding politician get together and dream up a cult. Started in Uganda in the 1980s, the Movement for the Restoration of the Ten Commandments of God does exactly what it says on the box – it advocates for the restoration of the Bible's Ten Commandments.

After years of hardship and turmoil, many people in Uganda were understandably looking for solace after living through war, a cruel dictatorship and economic hardship. While deserving of a break, what the people of Uganda got was the opposite. They got a cult run by a bunch of horrifically deranged humans with murderous intentions.

With five leaders sitting at the top, this cult followed the predictable paint-by-numbers formula of late 90s cults. There were visions of the Virgin Mary, claims of having direct contact with God, and a doomsday prophesy to coincide with the birth of the millennium. There were also some weird bans on life essentials (like sex and soap) and the customary practice of signing over all your property and wealth to the cult leaders for 'safe keeping'.

In news that may not come as a complete shock, the world did not end on January 1, 2000. Realising their bogus end-of-the-world predictions were stretching the credulity of their followers, the leaders of the Movement decided to end the world in their own special, psychotic way. On March 17, 2000, they lured their followers to a church, boarded up the exits and set fire to the building, killing more than 500 people inside, including themselves. A further investigation by authorities revealed more than 200 other bodies on other various properties belonging to the Movement.

With the final official death toll reaching a devastating 778 people, this mind-bogglingly depraved event is one of the biggest mass murders the world has ever seen. The leaders of the Movement for the Restoration of the Ten Commandments of God had obviously forgotten the commandments they so fervidly wanted to restore. 'Thou shalt not kill' ring any church bells, guys?

So, the Ten Commandments are a bit dated for your liking?

Good call, who's got time to follow such strict rules anyway? One of the main reasons mainstream religions are reporting declining numbers of followers is because of all the damn rules. No sex before marriage. No contraception. No stealing from the collection plate. Pfffft. It would be better for them to list the things you *are* allowed to do.

Thinking along these lines, sex has to be one of the biggest sticking points for most religions. Instead of viewing sexual pleasure as a healthy part of adult life, it's twisted into a shameful sin (unless of course the two people getting it on are married consenting adults, who are male and female, and only having sex with the intention to make a baby).

Do you believe that mainstream religion needs a lot more sex?

Absolutely. Everyone is so bloody repressed these days, bring on sexual liberation!

Find your cult on page 48

I'm not really bothered. I'm not asexual but it's not exactly the focus of my life either.

Turn to page 62 to keep searching

I'm a puritan all the way. I feel I was born in the wrong era.

Find your cult on page 58

You're now a member of ...

Gloriavale Christian Community

If you're a woman and you enjoy cooking, cleaning, child-rearing and marrying someone who may be a blood relative, you're in luck! You've just joined New Zealand's Gloriavale Christian Community, and you can forget about the existence of abstract concepts like higher education, marrying for love, building a business or travelling overseas. And you can absolutely forget your aspirations to become a burlesque performer. Why chase fulfilment from questionable activities like these when you can find enlightenment in domestic servitude? Remember: every diarrhoea-filled nappy you change brings you closer to God!

Located in New Zealand, the Gloriavale Christian Community is a 500-odd strong group of people blissfully unaware that it's 2016. Headed up by the aptly named Hopeful Christian (formerly known as Neville Cooper), Gloriavale has all the trappings of a fundamentalist Christian cult. Run by a man with a string of sex convictions to his name, members of Gloriavale are shut off from the outside world and live a highly controlled, ordered existence.

Established more than 45 years ago, Gloriavale is clearly stuck in one hell of a conservative time warp. Members live in a time where matching dresses and head scarves are the standard uniform and a woman giving birth to twelve or more children in her lifetime is considered the norm. With strict rules governing everything from what members can wear to who they can marry, people who live within Gloriavale don't have much free agency at all, because their life choices are not their own.

Brave members who have walked away from the cult have expressed genuine shock at finding out their pious leader once served time for sex offences. Strangely enough, many ex-members still hanker for the stress-free lifestyle they gave up in favour of living in the outside world. Let's face it, inside Gloriavale there are no taxes to pay, no raging Twitter arguments to fume over, no horror Tinder dates to run from and no hangovers to recover from. For many, Gloriavale really is heaven on earth.

You're clearly into palm trees, beaches and sunshine.

While many people associate cults with underground bunkers and secretive communes set up on ranches in the middle of nowhere, some cults operate right out in the open, in the most unexpected of places. That's right, cults don't discriminate when it comes to location, they also don't discriminate when it comes to socio-economic standing. Wealthy people join cults, as do middle-class folk and the unemployed.

Now, the British Royal Family might appear to be a strange segue here, but the royals have much more to do with cults than you'd think (and no, I'm not talking about Illuminati conspiracy theories).

So where do you stand on the monarchy?

I couldn't care less about the Royal Family.

Find your cult on page 66

It's a bit of a guilty pleasure, but I am a major Monarchist. From the unflappable Queen Elizabeth II, to everyone's favourite ginger-headed party boy Prince Harry, I won't hear a bad word spoken about the British Monarchy.

Find your cult on page 82

You're now a ...

Millerite

Get ready to step back into a time when New York was home to a hotbed of revivalist religious activity. That's right, in the early-to-mid 1800s, a sizeable chunk of the Big Apple was essentially one big bible study group, with Millerism standing out as one of the most memorable biblical movements to emerge from the scene at the time. As a follower of Millerism, you'll listen to the teachings (and preachings) of Baptist war veteran William Miller, who like many other cult leaders was prone to predicting the end of the world. And just like all the others who have predicted the cataclysm before (and after) him, it doesn't end well for anyone.

Proving that apocalyptic cults were around long before the heady days of the Y2K bug and the fizzer that was the end of the Mayan calendar back in 2012, Millerism was all over the Second Coming scene back in the mid 1800s.

Millerism was a movement dreamed up by a Massachusetts-born man named William Miller. Having seen action in the Battle of Plattsburgh, Miller turned to the Bible for solace and comfort. While studying the verses, Miller became a little obsessed with the Book of Daniel, especially Chapter Eight, which alludes to the end of the world. After some calculations, Miller predicted Christ's Second Coming would take place in 1843, and the cult of Millerism was born.

Operating from New York's 'burned-over district' (an area known for hosting a proliferation of religious revivals during this period of history), Miller hit the Baptist preacher trail, gathering crowds wherever he went. Like many other cult leaders, when the Second Coming failed to occur as Miller predicted, he just revised the timing of his prophesy, this time to a specific date in 1844. When his prophesy once again failed to come true, his followers were thrown into a wave of collective confusion and grief known as the 'Great Disappointment'. Having given away their possessions in preparation for the return of Christ, it's understandable that the Millerites were a little miffed at Christ's no-show.

While saddened that his predictions hadn't come to pass, Miller never stopped believing in the imminent return of Christ – a belief he held onto until his death in 1849. Miller's followers may have left him after the 'Great Disappointment', but many moved on to other sects and religions – such was the need to believe in something; anything. Some became Quakers, some became Shakers and others went on to form new movements with roots in Millerite beliefs, including the Seventh-day Adventist Church and the Bahá'í Faith, both of which still thrive today. While Miller got it wrong, he unknowingly ended up playing an integral part in the genesis of religions that many people still follow today.

You're now a ...

Juggalo

Paint your face to look like a deranged clown, light up a doobie and grab a can of Faygo soda, you're now a Juggalo (or Juggalette, if you're a woman). A super-fan of Detroit-based horrorcore-meets-hip hop masters Insane Clown Posse, as a Juggalo you don't just follow a genre of music. Oh no, being a Juggalo is a way of life – and a very fun one at that if you're into releasing anger at wild festivals and scaring the bejesus out of all the kids in your neighbourhood.

Rising to prominence in the 1990s, the Insane Clown Posse has managed to capture a unique demographic of fans who are keen on lapping up everything these oh-so angry clowns riff on. Proud of their working class origins, the Insane Clown Posse have fans from all walks of life claiming to be a part of the Juggalo subculture – from college drop-outs to washed-up celebrities desperate to maintain relevance.

So what makes someone a Juggalo?

Apart from being a fan of the Insane Clown Posse (and other bands operating under the Psychopathic Records label), Juggalos also have a penchant for drinking locally manufactured budget soda brand, Faygo. Typically, they wear clown face paint and attend the annual Gathering of the Juggalos Festival – a chaotic, Faygo-drenched four-day event characterised by an abundance of freaky costumes, nudity, drugs and Vanilla Ice (yep, Vanilla Ice identifies as a Juggalo).

Despised by many and written off as nothing more than a bunch of white-trash losers, it may be hard for outsiders to understand the allure of belonging to the Juggalo family. But the words of the Insane Clown Posse sum up the attraction:

We may paint our faces. We may fuck around. But pussy-ass bitches here won't be found. My homies stand behind me all the way. My true family and forever we'll stay. Don't fuck with me, cause they got my back. Where do your friends go, when they know you can't hack? Do they stay and help? Fuck no, they run! Back to their mommies while we have our fun. My Juggalo family, we don't fuck around. So tell me this now, are you down with the clown?

So essentially, as a Juggalo you get to play dress-ups all year long, drink soda like it's going out of fashion, indulge in every vice imaginable for four days of the year and revel in the comfort of belonging to a 'family' that's got your back, no matter what. You may have trouble finding a job but fuck it, you're a Juggalo – you're in good company.

Okay, so sex isn't a big drawcard for you.

Perhaps we've come on a bit too strong. Let's take it down a notch and start with some non-sexual physical contact.

How do you feel about hugs?

I love hugs! Hugs from strangers. Hugs from neighbours. Hugs from lovers. I'll take everything I can get.

Find your cult on page 32

I hate hugs. Hugging just isn't necessary, especially within religion. Get away from me!

Turn to page 12 to keep searching

Hugging? Meh. I can take it or leave it.

Turn to page 18 to keep searching

You're now a member of ...

The Cult That Cannot Be Named

Greetings earthling! Get your chequebook ready, you've just joined what may be the most litigious cult on planet Earth. Founded by a science fiction writer (who may or may not have believed that an alien called [**REDACTED**] brought humans to earth thousands of years ago), the Cult That Cannot Be Named has attracted its fair share of attention from everyone from the FBI to the *Daily Mail*. In order to be fair on the poor old [**REDACTED**] we have decided to censor parts of this book (and will cleverly avoid being bankrupted at the same time). Membership of this cult can go one of many ways. You could end up ostracised from your family, or wind up locked up in the 'Hole' (a compound protected by snipers and barbed wire) or you could end up being a Hollywood star prone to jumping on couches on talk shows. Either way, be prepared to part with a lot of money to be a part of [**REDACTED**].

In order to stay off this cult's extensive burn list and avoid a court date we can't afford, we'll just leave these clues here to help you work out who we're talking about:

- There is a whole *Wikipedia* page dedicated to cataloguing this cult's extraordinarily long history of dragging people (and being dragged by other people) into court.
- As a registered religious organisation, this cult has tax exempt status.
- According to tax documents, just two, small offshoots of this 'church' are worth more than $1.2 billion buckaroos combined.
- The wife of this cult's current leader hasn't been seen since 2006.
- Charles Manson once joined this cult then left because it was 'too crazy'.
- Wikipedia has banned this cult from updating pages on the website due to constant inaccurate, misleading updates.
- This cult isn't for commitment-phobes. When you sign up, your commitment is for a billion years.

You're now a member of ...

The John Frum Movement

Phew. You've joined one of the most harmless cults in the world. While many other cults are run by maniacal leaders hell-bent on pulling off doomsday suicide pacts, as a member of the John Frum Movement you won't have to deal with anyone trying to feed you cyanide-laced drinks, set fire to your compound or any of the other violent hallmarks of cult life. As a member of the John Frum Movement, you'll get to live in the South Pacific and drink a lot of kava. You'll also worship a white man you've never met, who probably never existed. In many ways, it's just like Christianity, but more fun.

A hangover from World War II, the elevation of a man named John Frum to God status is a classic example of what happens when an island culture receives a sudden injection of thousands of white strangers bearing gifts. From chocolate bars to cigarettes, cans of soda, shiny new Jeeps and more, many Pacific Island dwellers were first introduced to consumer goods and mass-produced foodstuffs thanks to an influx of American soldiers stationed in the area during World War II.

With a US military base being established in Port Vila, Vanuatu, thousands of American GIs rubbed shoulders and worked alongside locals, unknowingly creating the perfect storm for a 'cargo cult' to erupt into being. It was during this period in history that the John Frum movement started taking hold, with the movement causing so much of a stir that the US military dispatched Major Samuel Patten to the island in 1943, just to hose down the John Frum hysteria sweeping the area. His efforts were largely futile as the movement still exists today. You had one job Major Patten.

The movement is centred around the belief that one day a powerful American man named John Frum would shower an abundance of consumer goods on the island's people. It's unclear where the idea originated, or if Frum even existed, but offshoots of the John Frum movement sprung up all over the island. With locals creating makeshift spotting towers out of bamboo and cutting out airstrips for Frum to land his plane, the local people were only setting themselves up for disappointment: when the war ended, the American GIs left – taking their Coke bottles and candy bars with them.

Despite the American influx being so short-lived and John Frum continuing to ignore their prayers, the people of Tanna still celebrate 'John Frum Day' on February 15 each year. With locals dressing up in American military garb, many people on the island of Tanna still dream the impossible dream – that the American called John Frum will return and once again lavish them with chocolates, tobacco and appliances.

You're not following your nose or hearing any voices, so you're going to have to rely on another sense to find a cult that's your cup of tea, so to speak.

Surely by now, you're feeling pretty thirsty. Everyone needs a cool drink once in a while, so feel free to wet your whistle and let your choice lead you to enlightenment.

Hypothetical time: If you came across two pitchers containing two different brands of soda, which one would you drink?

I'd totally drink the Kool-Aid.
Or other, similar product.

Find your cult on page 72

I'd take a sip of Detroit's finest beverage, Faygo.

Find your cult on page 60

I would skip both and stay thirsty.
I would never sip random drinks of unknown origin, anything could be in there!

Turn to page 18 to keep searching

You're now a member of ...

Chen Tao

I hope you're a fan of wearing all-white matching ensembles, because you've just joined a cult that is more 90s than the 90s itself. There's matching uniforms (complete with cowboy hats), a belief in alien life and a prophecy about God returning to earth to save the chosen few (that's you!).

Your journey with Chen Tao will take you from Taiwan to Texas and back again, and while you won't gain much in the process, unlike many other cult members, you'll get to leave this one with your life. For a while there, you'll believe many outlandish things, but that's nothing that you won't recover from in time. We all believed in some outlandish shit in the 90s, you just went large with Chen Tao.

Originating in Taiwan, Chen Tao (or 'True Way') was a cult very much of its time. Like many other cults operating on the circuit during the late 90s (a pretty hectic era in the world of cults), the earth's impending move into the new millennium created the perfect, fearful conditions for the proliferation of doomsday cults to sweep the earth.

Operating under the name Chinese Soul Light Research Association and then God's Salvation Church, Chen Tao was a cult that merged the East with the West, and confused a hell of a lot of people in the process. A hybrid of Christianity and Buddhism (with a little intergalactic, extraterrestrial action thrown in to the mix to add some sci-fi appeal), Chen Tao followed the playbook of most other doomsday cults. There were predictions of a Second Coming, with God soon to be beamed into our lounge rooms via a television set (no cable subscription needed). Thousands of dollars changed hands between prophet and followers (to fund a journey off planet Earth via a spaceship disguised as a cloud, of course) and there was a move from Taiwan to Texas that managed to alarm many middle-class Americans living in the town of Garland, Dallas, who weren't too keen on their new neighbours who reportedly liked to get around in matching white suits and cowboy hats.

Like most doomsday cults, Chen Tao was doomed from the start. The founder of Chen Tao (a former Professor of Sociology at Chianan College of Pharmacology and Science) essentially made a bunch of stuff up and, when none of his predictions of God appearing on Channel 18 came true (shockingly enough), most people left the cult and returned to Taiwan.

What sets this cult apart from many others is that no one got hurt in the process. After God failed to show up on the Home Shopping Network, Hon-Ming Chen (the founder of Chen Tao) made himself available for stoning or crucifixion, but no one took him up on the offer. Most of the followers just left and resumed their Chen Tao-free lives somewhere else.

You're now a member of ...

The Peoples Temple Agricultural Project *AKA* 'Jonestown'

Ouch. You've just joined a cult responsible for the greatest predetermined loss of American life before September 11. As a member of this cult you'll live in a 'socialist paradise' in the South American country of Guyana, working twelve hours a day, six days a week, while helping to build an agricultural utopia. At night, you'll attend socialism classes and listen to lengthy talks on such thrilling subjects as the Soviet alliance. If this isn't disturbing enough, you'll then commit 'revolutionary suicide' by ingesting cyanide along with more than 900 others. The world will be collectively horrified at the macabre, surreal images of your body lying dead alongside hundreds of others in the jungle with colourful macaws looking on in innocent curiosity. Along with most of the world, your friends and family will mourn you and be left with nothing but questions. Why would a cult leader take the lives of so many? What was it all for? What madness led to this? And why did you drink the bloody Kool-Aid?

When it comes to the world of cults, what happened at Jonestown still rates as one of the nastiest events on public record (and that is something considering all the screwed up stuff that has happened in the world since the 1970s).

Headed up by a megalomaniacal American called Jim Jones, this cult built on socialist ideals was a bit of a controversy-magnet since its inception in California in the 1950s. But it wasn't until the 70s that things really started to kick off for the folk of the Peoples Temple. When Jones started copping heat from the media and authorities in California, he set his sights on the South American country of Guyana. Promising to set up a benevolent communist community for his followers, the relocation project soon descended into a terrifying ordeal for all involved.

With a notoriously unstable Jones abusing everything from Quaaludes to Valium and LSD, suffering from poor physical and mental health, and growing increasingly paranoid in response to intense scrutiny from the American government and the world's media, many relatives of cult members expressed grave concern over the welfare of their loved ones. And they were right to suspect something wasn't quite right with this super shady Jim Jones dude who had permanently glazed eyes and a penchant for peddling lies (Jones repeatedly claimed African-American and Native American heritage despite being white).

When a group of defectors realised what deep shit they were in, they tried to escape on a chartered flight arranged by the American government. Unfortunately, other members of the cult launched an attack on the airstrip killing five people and injuring eleven. While shocking, this was just a taster of what was to come.

Jim Jones' final act was so incredibly maniacal, it's still hard to understand. After whipping up a cocktail of Flavor Aid (not Kool-Aid) and Phenergan, cyanide and other neurotoxins, Jones summoned his followers, then incited them to ingest the deadly concoction (his speech was recorded and has become known as the 'Jonestown Death Tape'). That day, over 900 followers (including an astounding 300 children) died after drinking the potion, Jones included. It's difficult to know if the followers really knew what they were drinking, as there are so few survivors to give testimony. Whether they drank the potion knowing it would kill them but were too scared to say no, or were simply so brainwashed they were unable to make a conscious choice, Jim Jones was responsible for their murder or assisted suicide.

Tragic, and stranger than fiction, the Jonestown phenomenon is still deeply ingrained in our culture, with the phrase 'drinking the Kool-Aid' (even though it was actually Flavor-Aid) used to mean being brainwashed. Rock band Brian Jonestown Massacre are named after the incident, and, proving that nothing is sacred, you can buy 'Jonestown Family Fun Day' T-shirts (proudly sponsored by Kool-Aid).

Okay, it's totally understandable that you're not into the smell of sulphur.

Rotten egg gas is an acquired taste and generally only favoured by those deserving of eternal damnation. Perhaps you should rely on your ears to lead the way. Many cults use music to gain new followers, reach wider audiences and deliver sneaky subliminal messages. From frenetic chanting to devotional songs, music is the perfect medium to engage the masses.

While most people like music, tastes vary from person to person.

Are you a fan of psychedelic rock?

Yeah, man. Gimme all your LSD, too!

Find your cult on page 114

No. Psychedelic rock is so bad, people have to drop acid to endure it.

Turn to page 88 to keep searching

You're now a member of ...

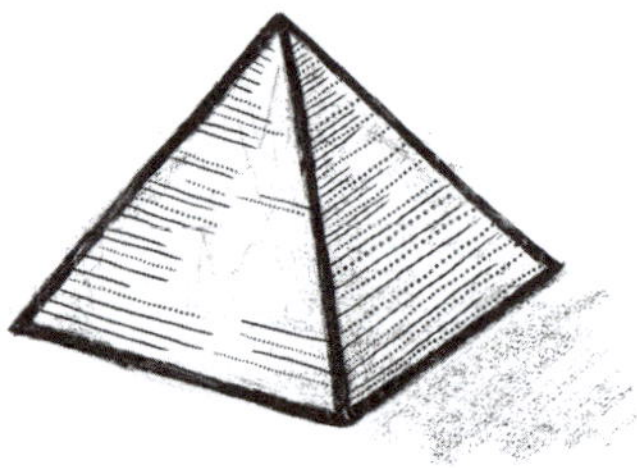

Amway

Welcome aboard, you're now an Amway representative. Your days will be spent flogging overpriced laundry powder to friends and family who may buy the odd product from you out of pity in the beginning, but eventually those pity-purchases will dry up as your friends grow tired of every catch-up being used as a prime opportunity for you to hit your sales targets. One day, you'll wake up with no friends and you'll have nothing to show for it but your 'Amway Employee of the Month' award and a laundry full of cleaning products that perform no better than a $1.00 bottle of white vinegar mixed with hot water.

Founded in 1959, Amway's direct-selling methods, church revivalist-style gatherings and pyramid scheme-like business model have landed the company in many courtrooms and newspapers over the decades.

Short for 'The American Way', Amway's multi-level marketing method allows sellers to not only earn income from their own sales, but also a percentage of the profits earned by all other Amway sellers that they've recruited. With this vested interest in both selling and recruiting, Amway's operating model has drawn many comparisons over the years to cult recruitment tactics.

Amway has been banned in China, investigated for illegal trading by the High Court in India, been found guilty of tax fraud in Canada and was stopped from operating in the UK by the Department of Trade and Industry. Amway was even sued by supermarket retail giant Proctor & Gamble after Amway representatives were caught spreading rumours that Procter & Gamble was run by Satanists.

Despite this, Amway still reports sales figures in the billions of dollars, almost 60 years after its creation. With strong links to the Republican Party, despite decades of controversy, lawsuits and criticism, Amway is still raking it in. It's the American Way!

You're now a member of ...

Heaven's Gate

Pack your bags, you've just scored a one-way ticket to paradise. As a member of the infamous Heaven's Gate cult you'll be believing in many wildly interesting things, foremost that an alien spaceship will visit earth by attaching itself to a comet called Hale-Bopp. While whizzing by Earth in the late 1990s, your extraterrestrial friends will beam you up before jetting off to eternity with your soul safely in hand. Yes, this is what you will believe and, sadly, you'll be willing to die for it.

While Heaven's Gate is only one of many UFO-cults, it certainly is the cream of the crop when it comes to modern absurdity. Co-founded by a middle-aged man called Marshall Applewhite in the 1970s, Heaven's Gate is the tragic intersection where mental illness and science fiction meet. Believing that Earth was on a collision course with destruction, Applewhite convinced believers that the only way to be saved was to shed all attachments to the human form. So goodbye money, jobs, sexuality, personality and anything else fun that would get in the way of reaching nirvana.

Unlike many other cult leaders, Applewhite *knew* he was mentally unstable, reportedly often checking himself into mental-health facilities over the years. Among the many bizarre features of life within Heaven's Gate, Applewhite and some other members voluntarily submitted to castration (to remove sexual desire) and even took out an insurance policy against being abducted and impregnated by aliens.

Ultimately, life in Heaven's Gate doesn't end well. In 1997, 40 members of the cult committed mass suicide in a mansion in San Diego. Eating applesauce laced with barbiturates, followed by a vodka chaser, the group tied plastic bags over their heads to ensure asphyxiation in case the heavy spirit and sedative cocktail didn't do the trick. If that's not enough, they all died wearing matching leisurewear – a fetching ensemble of sweatpants, complete with pairs of matching black and white Nikes and a commemorative armband emblazoned with the words 'Heaven's Gate Away Team'. Luggage neatly packed and waiting alongside their corpses when emergency services arrived days later, no one can accuse the Heaven's Gate crew of not being prepared for their intergalactic trip to infinity and beyond.

Thanks to a clever succession plan, the Heaven's Gate cult apparently still operates today, with active members reportedly waiting for the next spaceship pickup from a compound in France's Pyrenees mountains. Meanwhile, the Heaven's Gate website is still active in all its 1990s web design glory (best viewed in Netscape Navigator, of course). The question remains: who on Earth is continuing to pay the domain name registration fees?

While certainly a horrifying concept, a belief in the End of Days is a common thread linking many cults (and woeful disaster movies) over the years.

Whether it's a primal desire to stick with the herd when the shit finally goes down, or a clever way to hedge bets just to make sure you end up on the right side of things, many cults attract people who are fearful of being alone when the world burns.

In your opinion, how will the world end?

An ecological disaster. → Find your cult on page 98

Aliens will come and destroy everything but save all the good people. → Find your cult on page 34

I'm not sure how, but it's going to happen and I do not want to be around to see it. → Find your cult on page 122

You're now a member of ...

The Prince Philip Movement

Congratulations, you've won a trip to sunny Vanuatu! You'll now get to spend the rest of your days lying in a hammock basking in golden sunshine while you sip coconut juice. But your entry to the Pacific paradise of Vanuatu comes with strings attached: as a member of the Prince Philip Movement you'll also have to believe that the Duke of Edinburgh is a divine being. Yes, you read that correctly. The Grand Master of the highly inappropriate comment and long-time sufferer of foot-in-mouth-disease Prince Philip is actually worshipped as a god by your new community, the Yaohnanen people from the island of Tanna.

In a rare slice of colonial absurdity, this bizarre cult is just one of the so-called 'cargo cults' that Vanuatu is home to. The genesis of the cult is reportedly linked to an ancient story of a local mountain spirit who once travelled overseas to faraway lands to marry a queen. When local villagers learned about Prince Philip after his visit to Port Vila in the 1970s, it made sense that he indeed was their mountain spirit, and he should be worshipped accordingly. Obviously, it appears that the story resonated with the locals because here we are a whole four decades later with Prince Philip continuing to enjoy God status by many villagers.

As far as cults go, this has got to be one of the better groups to join as, unlike many other cults, the Prince Philip Movement is gloriously free of mind control, mass murder and doomsday suicide pacts. All you have to do is live on a Pacific island and revere a rich, old codger prone to blurting out inflammatory racist jokes every now and then.

While we'd all like to think that we're evolved enough to not worry about trivial things like appearances, sometimes it's okay to admit to being superficial.

Aesthetics are important to many people and there's no point joining a cult if the uniform is fugly. White robes get dirty really quickly and garish colours don't suit all complexions. Choosing a cult that has the right garb for your body type is incredibly important and, quite frankly, I'm shocked that *Vogue* has never done a six-page spread on cult fashion for their annual bumper September issue.

If you had a choice between wearing one of four outfits, every day for the rest of your life, what would you choose?

A brown dressing gown. → Find your cult on page 96

A white-on-white suit ensemble with matching cowboy hat. → Find your cult on page 70

A bright orange kaftan. → Find your cult on page 42

Gross, I'd rather go naked than wear any of these. → Turn to page 106 to keep searching

Sweatpants and vintage 90s Nikes. → Find your cult on page 78

You're now a member of ...

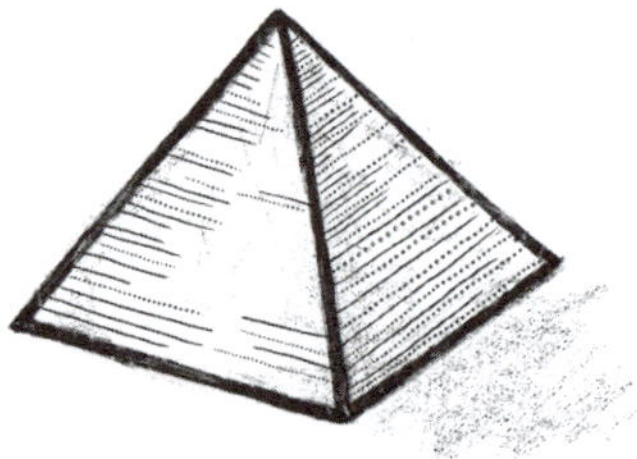

The town of Cults, Aberdeen

Well, well, well. Well done. You've managed to make it through this book without belonging to any cult. You've avoided joining satanic, animal-sacrificing cults in Mexico; just missed out on belonging to a sect that believes that humanity is descended from alien life; and dodged joining a cult that believes that Prince Philip is God. You obviously need answers beyond what this book can give you. You clearly need to go on a spiritual journey to find yourself. But where do you go to find peace, love and enlightenment? India? Bali? Nope. You're off to Scotland.

With a population of just over 3500 people, the town of Cults is located in Aberdeen, Scotland. While distinctly lacking in cultish activity, by all accounts the golf-themed Cults Hotel does a good roast on a Sunday. A grey village with absolutely nothing notable to hang its hat on, Cults is the perfect place to sit and have a long think about the gaping spiritual void you feel in your heart. While many take the well-trodden path to the ashrams of Rishikesh to seek enlightenment, you will spend your time in cold, grey Cults. Each year, thousands of other precious little snowflakes believe they will find oneness amid the green smoothies, acai bowls, colonic irrigation and bastardised yoga classes of Bali, but you will 'do the work' in Cults because you know that spiritual enlightenment can be attained anywhere ... even in Scotland.

Oh, so you don't like 26-minute songs filled with layers of fuzzy guitar accompanied by sitar, synth, unintelligible lyrics and an overdose of studio reverb?

Fair enough. Perhaps you are after something a little more pure. What about the raw power of the human voice? Many cults believe that chanting is a way to get closer to God, to purify the body and soul, and release negative energy. Having someone repeat the same phrase over and over again is also a pretty convenient method of brainwashing, but we'll just leave that thought with you.

With that in mind, what do you think of chanting?

I love it! Sign me up. → Find your cult on page 38

Ohmmmmmmmm ... Nope. → Turn to page 68 to keep searching

You're now a member of ...

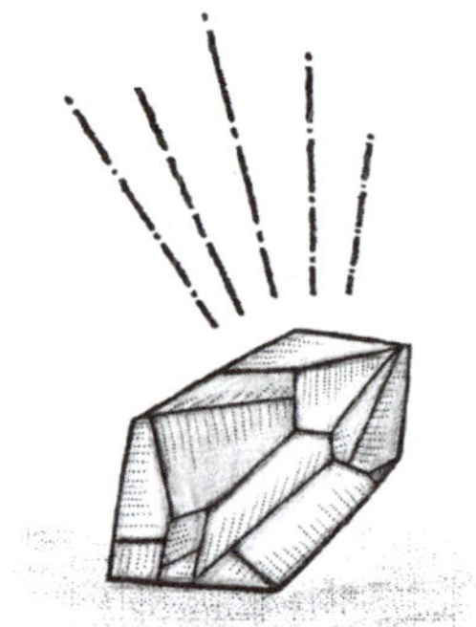

The Aetherius Society

Pack your favourite crystal, don your best ceremonial robes and brush up on your mantras, you're about to go on a very important cosmic mission with the Aetherius Society. As a member of this New Age cult with headquarters in London and Los Angeles (and chapters everywhere from Toronto to Lisbon) you'll believe in a little bit of everything from the woo-woo melting pot: from telepathy to reincarnation and the existence of extraterrestrial life forms. You'll participate in pilgrimages to holy mountains, healing circles and some pretty intense power prayer sessions characterised by dynamic movement, chanting and, of course, communication with aliens and beings living on other spiritual planes.

The Aetherius Society was founded by an Englishman named George King in 1955. After growing up in a Christian household, King turned to the esoteric and spiritual world, laying the foundations of what was to become the Aetherius Society. After a stint driving taxis in London, King set up the society and seemingly threw in every New Age cliché known to humankind. Meditation? Tick. Yoga? Tick? Channelling of cosmic masters? Tick. Telepathy? Tick.

King then went one step further and added some truly outrageous elements to the cosmic mix including claims that the universe is actually run by an interplanetary council of spiritual beings consisting of Jesus, Buddha and other masters. He was also quite liberal with the addition of titles to his name, with his 'official' title reported to be, 'His Eminence Sir George King, O.S.P., Ph.D., Th.D., D.D., Metropolitan Archbishop of the Aetherius Churches'*. Not bad for a taxi driver from Shropshire.

Some of the beliefs of this cult may seem ludicrous but when considering the absurd beliefs that mainstream religions espouse (certain humans can walk on water, part the sea, turn water into wine and come back from the dead), the Aetherius Society's chosen beliefs aren't *that* different. Considering this cult still has thousands of active members all over the world (despite King dying two decades ago), there's obviously demand for a religion that includes aliens in its holy tenet.

As far as cults go, this one is pretty harmless. This group hasn't been responsible for any mass suicides or murders, neither has it been linked to polygamy, forced marriage of children, abuse or tax fraud. They've fought no bloody wars in the name of God and haven't beaten and tortured others who choose to believe something different. By all accounts, the people of the Aetherius Society just want to spend their time directing their spiritual energy towards the healing of the world and, gawd knows, we need it.

* Titles may or may not have been earned. Let's just say they probably weren't.

You're now a member of ...

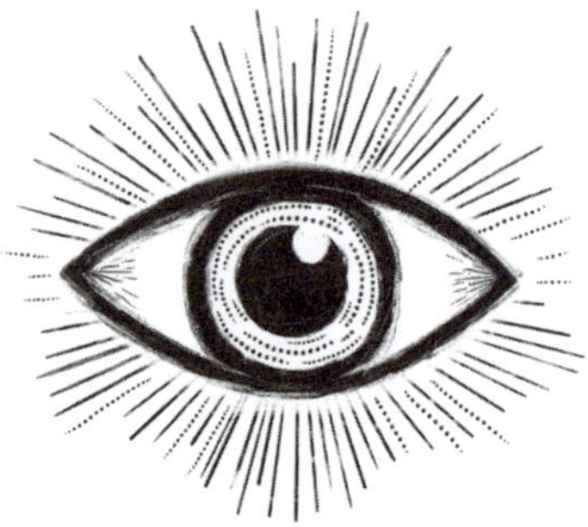

Landmark Worldwide

Do you feel that you are broken and in need of fixing? Do you think you could be leading a happier, shinier, more productive, more kick-ass life than your current, oh-so beige existence? Do you like being locked in a room and bullied for hours on end without a bathroom break while watching strangers sob on stage in front of hundreds of other strangers? Hope so, because you've just joined Landmark Worldwide, a self-improvement program that strays into cult territory thanks to aggressive recruitment tactics and strict rules of engagement for participants.

People touched by Landmark typically fall into one of two camps: you'll either love it or hate it. If you end up on the 'love it' side of the fence, after Landmark you'll report all sorts of amazing feats in your private life, from promotions at work to finding the partner of your dreams. You'll also begin ranting to your friends about Landmark with the gusto of a television evangelist. If you hate it, you'll walk away feeling nothing more than anger at being duped out of more than 500 bucks for three days of self-improvement waffle you could have easily found for free in any self-help section of your local public library. Welcome to Landmark.

Labelled a cult by the French government, 'one of the most dangerous sects in Sweden' by anti-cult support groups, and compared to old-fashioned snake oil peddlers by many, Landmark is no stranger to controversy. As a for-profit organisation, Landmark has also clocked up a lot of courtroom time, with the group choosing to litigate against detractors (a classic, overly aggressive manoeuvre used by many cults prone to reputation-management problems). They're also adept at withdrawing cases once the harsh reality that you can't litigate against everyone who doesn't like you sets in (something that the ... Cult That Cannot Be Named is yet to learn).

The history of Landmark is long and pretty boring, so all you need to know is that in its original form, the idea of Landmark was apparently concocted up by a used-car salesmen (not the most noble of professions to ever walk the earth). These days, Landmark Worldwide reports an annual revenue of over US$70 million from its programs that focus on encouraging personal responsibility and accountability (ugh).

While many claim that Landmark is nothing more than a cult that uses brainwashing and coercive tactics to entrap vulnerable people into parting with their money, many others report genuine, life-changing transformations as a result of attending a Landmark Forum. So, no one seems to know if Landmark is a cult, a scam or just a bog-standard pyramid scheme that has managed to gain remarkable traction. Either way, when you join Landmark your life changes. Whether it changes for better or worse – according to Landmark – is up to you.

It's time to talk about the concept of kinship.

For many, family means the people you are biologically related to (or married to). For others, a sense of family is more about being with folk who share similar ideals, beliefs, experiences, values and even deadly obsessions.

So, which side of the fence do you sit on when it comes to family?

I believe that you can create a family with whoever you like. Family is about bonds, not biology.

Find your cult on page 108

There is only one family and it's the one you were born into.

Turn to page 112 to keep searching

Who cares about family?
I'm here to live my best life. It's all about *self*-improvement.

Find your cult on page 92

You're now a member of ...

The Church of the Latter-Day Dude

Dude! You've just hit the spiritual jackpot by joining one of the coolest, cruisiest cults on the planet. As a member of the Church of the Latter-Day Dude most of your days will be spent taking it easy. You'll go bowling, drink a White Russian, maybe smoke some weed and shake off the haters by saying, 'Well, that's just your opinion man.' With a penchant for wearing a dressing gown in public, you'll live a life free of status anxiety and the dogged pursuit of achievement, because you are the Dude, His Dudeness, Duder, El Duderino.

Described as the 'slowest-growing religion in the world', Dudeism is a way of life underpinned by the philosophy espoused by 'The Dude' (played masterfully by Jeff Bridges) in the Coen Brothers' cult film *The Big Lebowski*. The Dude's philosophy of embracing laziness struck a chord with everyone from college kids to middle-aged dads, creating a worldwide cult of people who collectively embraced taking their foot off the pedal of life, in favour of letting things flow, man.

Considering that the church claims that the term 'dude' is gender-neutral and can be applied to anyone of any age or sex, this might just be one of the most inclusive cults in the world. With more than 350,000 ordained priests operating around the world, most US states now allow a 'Dude Priest' to legally officiate at funerals and weddings.

With links to Taoist philosophy, the Day of the Dude is celebrated globally on March 6. On this day, followers of Dudeism can do whatever the hell they want, which makes it just like any other day for them, really. Chilling out is almost certainly on the agenda, with a side order of accepting life as it comes, followed by a chaser of not taking life so seriously.

While many might mistakenly believe that Dudeism is nothing more than a gag-religion, the Church of the Latter-Day Dude has taken a public stance on important issues that impact the community. As a supporter of marriage equality, Dudeism is doing a much better job of loving our fellow dudes than the Catholic Church and most other mainstream religions ever have or likely will. When it comes to tapping into what people want out of religion these days, the Dude most certainly abides.

You're now a member of ...

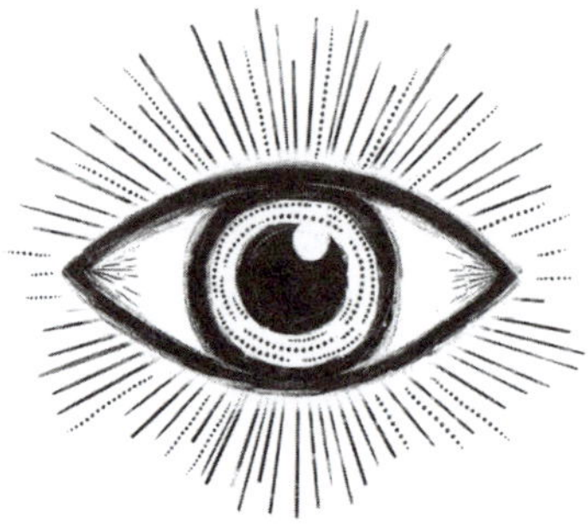

The Congregation for the Light

The good news is that you've joined a cult based in the midtown area of Murray Hill, Manhattan (you're off to New York, baby). The bad news is that you've joined a small, secretive doomsday cult with homophobic tendencies and a belief in the Aryan 'master race'. Ouch. As a member of the Congregation for the Light, you'll spend your time training for an ecological disaster that will herald the end of the world, so you'll be ready to roll when the end-of-days shit goes down. Which is apparently any day now according to the Congregation for the Light.

Part cult, part secret society, the Congregation for the Light proves that the southern states of the USA don't have a stranglehold on cult activity. From its home in a brownstone in New York, New York, the spiritual headquarters of this cult are hidden in plain view in one of the world's busiest and most progressive cities. Make no mistake, this cult is a cut above other groups that operate from sad, run-down compounds on farms in backwater states no one else wants to live in. These guys have invested in prime real estate for its 200-or-so members to meet.

While the Congregation for the Light had been going about its creepy, secret business since the 1970s with no one so much as raising an arched brow, it was only when exiled, ex-members started spilling their guts to the tabloids in 2014 that New Yorkers started to take note. With former members informing the media that the group's core belief is in an Aryan super race hailing from Atlantis, the public suddenly got *very* interested in this kooky cult.

With ex-members revealing that homosexuality is forbidden, corporal punishment of children is encouraged and female members are denied higher education in favour of being married off to old dudes (why does this never play out in reverse?), the Congregation for the Light certainly ticks off all the usual cult boxes, namely: creepy old dude as figurehead, doomsday predictions that never come true, and victimisation and abuse of vulnerable, marginalised people. 'For the light'? Sure ...

Ahhh, so you're one of those UFO-spotting types.

Good on you for being open to the existence of other life forms. Surely our solar system harbours all sorts of beings beyond humanity, so it makes sense to look towards aliens when it comes to spirituality. Luckily, there are a whole range of alien-worship cults out there. While many of these cults consist of members who are average Joes, many have also nabbed celebrities in their worship web, and some routinely recruit stars to boost their profile.

Do you feel that you could have been a great actor but were never given the right platform?

Yes! I could've been a contender! → Find your cult on page 14

No. Don't you know the camera adds ten pounds? → Turn to page 40 to keep searching

I am totally already a Hollywood movie star. → Find your cult on page 64

You're now a member of ...

The Church of Satan

I hope you're okay with being damned for eternity, because you've just joined the Church of Satan! As a member of this devil-worshipping cult you'll totally freak out your family, friends and neighbours by signing over your soul to the light-bringer himself, Lucifer. You'll read up on such classics as *The Satanic Bible* and *Letters from the Devil*, perform rituals involving naked people and pentagrams, and of course, you'll wear a lot of black. As far as cults go, you've joined one of the cheapest and easiest to join, with lifetime membership coming pretty cheap at US$200 (plus whatever price you put on your soul).

Like so many other cults, the Church of Satan was established in San Francisco in the late 1960s. Operating from a residential building known as 'The Black House', the cult was created by an enterprising Satanist called Anton LaVey who came to be known in the media as the 'Father of Satanism'. As the founding father of modern Satanism, LaVey had a gift for ceremony, honed from years of performing music. He also had a talent for spinning wild, unsubstantiated yarns including tales of working as a 'psychic investigator' and once bedding Marilyn Monroe in his youth.

Author of many satanic texts still used by Satanists worldwide, Anton LaVey passed away in the late 90s. Proving that Satan never really dies, the Church of Satan didn't end with LaVey's death – it simply underwent new management and moved its headquarters to the most obvious place in the world: Hell's Kitchen in New York City. Modern Satanists are still encouraged to avoid committing the Nine Satanic Sins that LaVey wrote of decades ago, including: Pretentiousness, Solipsism, Self-deceit, Herd Conformity, Lack of Perspective, Forgetfulness of Past Orthodoxies, Counterproductive Pride and Lack of Aesthetics and Stupidity (considered the cardinal sin of Satanism).

Of course, Satanic worship has been around for centuries, but over the years Satan got organised, with the church benefitting from the rise of the machine. Yep, even old Beelzebub has a website now. With a lack of church buildings or other dedicated spaces for communities to meet, the Church of Satan encourages an individualist approach by simply asking members to sign up online, pay their fees via PayPal and get about worshipping in whatever (legal) way they see fit. While many cults shun modern technology and demand that members hole themselves up on rural properties in the backwaters of godforsaken places, Satanism is truly with the times. Simply click, pay and start devil-worshipping today!

You're now a member of ...

The Church of the Flying Spaghetti Monster

Fingers crossed you're not gluten-intolerant, as you've just joined a cult with very strong ties to the glorious act of eating pasta. With followers all over the world, this cult doesn't have many rules or require much of its members. There is no joining fee or commitment ceremony, nor is there any particular criteria for joining. Simply, the only thing required of members is to spread the good word about Pastafarianism in whatever peaceful way they can. So, all you need to do to become a good Pastafarian is wear a colander on your head, get out there on the evangelical trail and preach up a pasta-storm. Some churches have pastors, this church has pasta.

Called FSM for short, the Church of the Flying Spaghetti Monster's origins lie in a letter written by an American man named Bobby Henderson back in 2005. Addressed to the Kansas School Board, the letter was written in protest against the boards' decision to allow students to attend 'intelligent design' (aka creationism) classes as an alternative to learning about evolution. By demanding the school board acknowledge the Flying Spaghetti Monster as creator of the world (despite there being no evidence), Henderson was able to highlight the ridiculousness of teaching intelligent design alongside science.

For a cult that claims it has no ties to atheism and never intended to highlight the absurd impacts religious groups have on modern society, FSM does an incredibly good job of lampooning mainstream religions. Published in 2006, *The Gospel of the Flying Spaghetti Monster* won acclaim from many for explaining the philosophy and teachings of FSM.

With FSM being legally recognised as a bona fide religion in New Zealand and the Netherlands, this cult has won favour with many people beyond frat boys and girls. Many people around the world have successfully had official driver's license and identity card photos taken with colanders on their head. But for every person allowed to don a pasta strainer, many more are denied by governments and councils who refuse to recognise FSM as a religion. With this in mind, many Pastafarians are still fighting to gain acceptance within the greater community. For Pastafarians, the struggle is real.

People have been citing the influence of past lives as the reason for all types of behaviour for, well, probably as long as lives have been around.

Despite there being zero evidence of its existence – let alone its ability to impact the behaviour of people in their 'current' lives – the idea of reincarnation stubbornly refuses to go away. It's interesting to note that most people who claim to have lived past lives also happen to have been highly influential people in their previous incarnation. Ever noticed that people always claim to have been a pharaoh, queen or freedom fighter, rather than a cleaner, accountant or dental assistant? Hmmm ...

Do you have the sneaking suspicion that you have been here before?

Yes, I totally lived in Ancient Egyptian times. → Find your cult on page 132

Yes, I was a high priestess with special powers. → Find your cult on page 44

Yes, I am pretty sure I was an alien. → Find your cult on page 90

No, reincarnation is BS. → Turn to page 94 to keep searching

You're now a member of ...

The Manson Family

Get ready for your time in the limelight, you've just joined a group headed up by one of the most infamous cult leaders in the world. You come to join the Manson Family after a chance meeting with a small-statured, ex-con called Charles Manson. He seems a little weird, but you're in California during the Summer of Love and you're all about going wherever life takes you. Unfortunately, as a member of the Manson Family, life will take you straight to the slammer, which is exactly where you belong due to the utterly abhorrent crimes you commit in the name of your beloved leader, little Charlie Manson.

Shooting to worldwide fame for all the wrong reasons in the late 60s, the Manson Family story serves as a cautionary tale about trusting men who have nothing to offer but decades of prison time, shoddy home-tattooing skills and some very tenuous connections to the local music scene.

Started by Charles Manson, this cult may have been small, but what it lacked in size it more than made up for with ferocity. After spending more than half his life behind bars for a laundry list of crimes, including everything from car theft to pimping and forgery, Manson set his sights on becoming a famous musician. After writing and recording a series of tunes (and meeting Dennis Wilson from the Beach Boys), Manson started to think that his life was going to turn around.

A keen student of Dale Carnegie's *How to Win Friends and Influence People*, which he read in prison, Manson soon gained a group of mainly female followers. They lived together on a hippie commune in California where everyone would sit around in a purple haze, listening to Charlie wax lyrical about the impending race war that was due to hit earth anytime soon (according to Manson, the lyrics to the Beatles song 'Helter Skelter' clearly spell this out).

Sadly, the whole music thing didn't seem to work out for Charlie, but at least he still had guru-status with his small group of loyal followers. Disgruntled about his stalled music career, Manson planned his deadly vengeance on the society that had spurned him, but instead of going on a murder spree himself, he decided to let others do the dirty work for him.

Over the course of a few weeks in mid-1969, members of the Manson Family murdered eight people in different locations around Los Angeles, including the heavily pregnant Hollywood actress Sharon Tate, in a series of gruesome crimes that shocked the world. The Family members responsible for committing the murders ended up receiving death sentences, which were all later commuted to life imprisonment following the abolishment of the death penalty in the state of California.

While Manson didn't physically kill any of the victims, it was universally accepted that as the leader of the cult, he had been solely responsible for inciting and arranging the savage murders, in which people were shot, stabbed and bayonetted. Currently incarcerated with a life sentence, it's reported that Manson has received more fan mail than anyone else in the US prison system.

You're now a member of ...

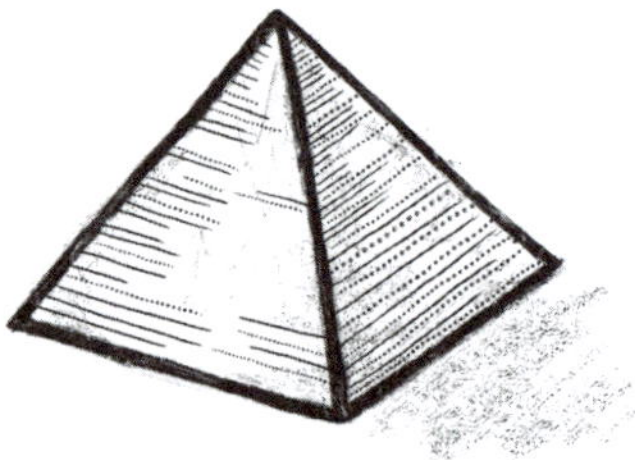

Eckankar

Hello soul traveller, you've just signed up to experience the light and sound of the Lord as a 'co-worker with God'. As a member of Eckankar, you'll chant mantras, sing songs, meditate and contemplate your way to spiritual liberation and self-realisation. And you'll get to do all this while living a relatively normal life, wherever you like, because in Eckankar there's no hiding away in weird compounds on farms in the middle of nowhere. Nope, there's none of that. Instead, you'll work, study, live and love as usual – you'll just also worship a god called Sugmad (who is neither female nor male) while making sure your slate is kept clean, as Eckists believe that karma is a bitch and your bad deeds will come and bite you on the ass at some point. Despite this, Eckists don't believe in the idea of original sin, so at least you've joined one of the less preachy cults out there.

Founded in the mid 1960s by an American freelance journalist from Kentucky called Paul Twitchell, Eckankar has steadily grown to become a worldwide phenomenon.

In the beginning, Eckankar's head office was located in Las Vegas – because where better to obliterate bad karma than in Sin City? With its new spiritual headquarters (called the Temple of ECK) now located in Minnesota, Eckankar has hundreds of branches all over the world. From Thailand to Togo, Scotland to Sweden, Eckankar followers can be found almost everywhere.

Making serious moolah from membership fees, seminars and donations (especially generous bequeathments from deceased members), Eckankar is a pretty switched-on organisation with a strong social media presence, slick branding and an impressive postmodern temple for members to visit. Followers are encouraged to let their soul travel in the form of astral projection or lucid dreaming, in order to reach a higher plane and find spiritual freedom.

While it's anyone's guess why Eckankar is still going strong after more than five decades, there's something to be said for its non-threatening, non-judgemental approach to worship and spiritual enlightenment. Members simply sign up for an annual membership and commit to some pretty easy mantra meditation. In a world where everyone has collectively turned into massive commitment-phobes, Eckankar has tapped into a formula that works for modern folk who don't want to be pinned down in case something better comes up.

Of course, Eckankar has its detractors, with reports of ex-Eckankar folk finding it hard to leave due to fear of accruing bad karma, but what's refreshing about Eckankar is that there doesn't seem to be many of the dogmatic rules that so many other cults and mainstream religions are so keen on. Sexual orientation and reproductive rights are not the types of things Eckankar cares about and likewise they don't give a brass razoo about your race, skin colour or choice of dress.

And here's the real kicker: you don't even have to renounce your religion to join.

Many cults require members to cast off all their worldly possessions, while others ask followers to sign over all their money and property to a cult leader for 'safekeeping'.

And some groups get their followers to work for free in multimillion-dollar businesses registered to the cult.

How do you think people should use their personal income?

Money should be spent on consumer goods. Ideally, they should be purchased from friendly direct sellers who visit your home.

Find your cult on page 76

I think that a person's income should be handed over to a supreme being who can be trusted to distribute the funds as needed.

Find your cult on page 10

All income should be pooled and shared with the community. No one needs to go without if everyone shares their resources.

Find your cult on page 128

People should spend their money freely. After all, you can't take it with you when you die!

Turn to page 130 to keep searching

You're now a member of ...

The Source Family

Get ready to get groovy baby, you've just joined one of the most intriguing cults to come out of America in the 1960s. As a member of the Source Family, you'll follow a World War II veteran named James Edward Baker (also known as 'Father Yod'). You'll also change your last name to Aquarian and split your time between working in the cult's popular health-food restaurant on the Sunset Strip and gigging in the cult's experimental psychedelic rock band Ya Ho Wa 13. At night, you'll retire to a cosy three-bedroom commune located in the Hollywood Hills, where you'll bunk down with up to 150 other Source Family members.

With its strange-named, long-haired leader with fourteen wives and a penchant for psychedelic rock; white-robed, vegetarian followers interested in Eastern mysticism; and America's first health-food restaurant popular with the likes of John Lennon and Yoko Ono – cults don't get much more '60s California' than the Source Family.

Unfortunately, the heat was well and truly turned up on Father Yod and his followers after Charles Manson and his merry little family went on their murderous rampage. The Source Family decamped to Hawaii to escape the scrutiny, but life in paradise didn't last long for Father Yod. Despite having no experience in the sport, he died after attempting to hang-glide off a cliff in a #YOLO moment gone wrong. Cue: Bon Jovi's 'Blaze of Glory'.

Without Father Yod at the helm, the Source Family disbanded and the followers had to get used to the harsh realities associated with living a 'normal' life. The Source Family were largely forgotten about by the masses until a documentary called *The Source Family* debuted at Austin's South by Southwest Film Festival in 2012. You know you've made it as a cult leader when a documentary about your life makes a splash at one of America's most influential independent film festivals, and Father Yod promptly gained a whole new legion of fans. In death, as in life, Father Yod is still hip with the kids.

The Source Family sheds light on the bizarre antics of a man who seemingly lived a thousand lives even before becoming a cult leader, and makes a strong case that truth is most certainly always stranger than fiction.

You're now a member of ...

Los Narco-Satánicos

Sorry, but this is bad. Really, really bad. You've just joined a Mexican drug cartel responsible for the gruesome murders of more than twenty five people. As a member of this cult, you'll believe that a drug kingpin-cum-cult leader called Adolfo Constanzo has the power to ward off evil spirits and guarantee safe passage of drug shipments simply by casting magic voodoo spells picked up while on childhood trips to Haiti. Pity that these spells don't work. Double pity that these spells involve killing and mutilating people and animals. When it comes down to it, there's no easy way to say this except that you've just joined one of the most evil, sadistic, nasty cults to ever exist in the history of this twisted world. Well done, sicko.

There's a reason why Adolfo Constanzo regularly features on the media's 'most evil' lists. Even though he shot to fame in the late 80s, his name still sends shivers down the spine of anyone who was unlucky enough to come across him.

Despite what Netflix tells you, operating a drug cartel in Mexico isn't as cool as it looks. There's lots of stakeholder management required, what with rival cartels, the authorities, concerned locals and staff to deal with – all while trying to shift units of the finest narcotics to the world. Drug runner Adolfo came up with a novel way to ensure that his business flourished in a highly competitive environment. He simply turned to black magic – because who needs a business plan when you've got a cauldron and a dead goat?

Known as the Godfather of Matamoras, Adolfo, having apprenticed at a young age to a local sorcerer, created a nifty little business sacrificing animals for rich drug kingpins and hitmen keen on receiving a little extra help with their business. Yet, like most showmen, Adolfo felt the need to one-up each effort. When animal sacrifice wasn't enough, he started to raid graveyards for human bones. When the graveyard raiding became too hard, he decided that it was time to start getting involved in the human sacrifice game.

Moving to an isolated desert compound called Rancho Santa Elena, Adolfo and his followers started performing ritualistic torture and sacrifice of humans. They also started stockpiling cocaine and marijuana. With Adolfo's followers believing him to possess superpowers in witchcraft, they went out in search of people to bring to the ranch to feed his never-ending need for new sacrifices. In the beginning, they focused on the most vulnerable members of the society (homeless people and prostitutes), but they also 'sacrificed' other drug cartel leaders as a way of eliminating the competition.

It's anyone's guess how long this utterly depraved behaviour would have gone on for, had it not been for a chance meeting with an American student. The cult unravelled once Adolfo's henchmen kidnapped and killed an unfortunate American spring breaker called Mark Kilroy. A massive search for the missing student eventually lead the authorities to the ranch, where they found torture dungeons, mutilated bodies, and cauldrons containing human body parts and a dead black cat.

Fleeing the bordertown of Matamoras, Adolfo and his followers ended up in Mexico City, but they didn't last long before being found by the authorities. Like a true cult leader, Adolfo couldn't face the music and begged to be shot by his followers (a request that they obliged). The remaining cult members were taken into custody and imprisoned after trial. And thus ended one of the world's nastiest cults. Good riddance.

Mainstream religions often enforce dietary rules on followers, from vegetarianism and veganism, to avoiding pork and dairy.

Just like registered religious organisations, many cults also dictate what followers can and cannot eat.

Do you think that carbs should be restricted in order to live a healthy lifestyle?

Yes. Carbohydrates convert to sugars and make us fat. → **Find your cult on page 16**

No way! Live by the carb, die by the carb. → **Find your cult on page 104**

Eat everything in moderation! → **Turn to page 84 to keep searching**

You're now a member of ...

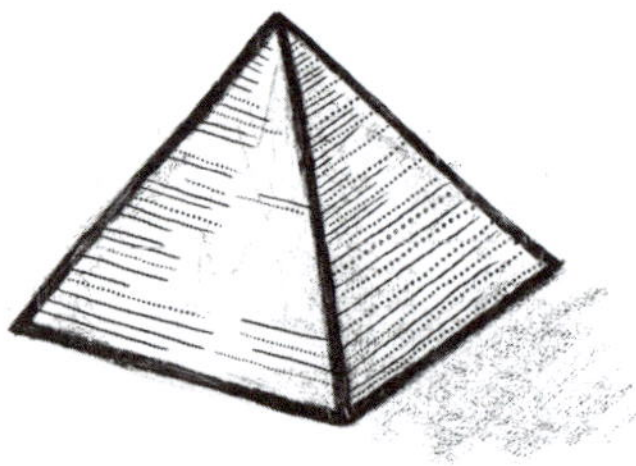

Aum Shinrikyo

Konichiwa! You've just joined a bizarre Japanese cult responsible for one of the most shocking acts of domestic terrorism on Japanese soil. As the group who carried out the 1995 Tokyo subway sarin gas attacks (as well as many other insanely cruel acts against humans and animals), Aum Shinrikyo probably won't offer you a lot of fun times. Realistically, you'll essentially only have two choices: leave and be murdered by other cult members or stay and be part of a group that murders strangers for no good reason. Check, mate!

Part cult, part political party, part terrorist organisation, Aum Shinrikyo was headed up by an enterprising visually-impaired man called Shoko Asahara. After studying traditional Chinese medicine, Shoko officially registered Aum Shinrikyo in 1987 and soon after began claiming to be Christ (it's that easy).

Aum Shinriyko was based on an unholy mess of ideas. Cherry-picking Buddhist and Christian beliefs, then mixing them with a mish mash of wild conspiracy theories involving everyone from the Royal Family to the Freemasons, Shoko also threw in a few doomsday predictions about World War III to keep things interesting.

After testing deadly sarin gas on unsuspecting livestock at a property in a remote part of Western Australia (resulting in the death of many sheep) the group launched an attack on the Tokyo subway system, apparently in an attempt to overthrow the Japanese emperor. It's unclear how unleashing toxic gas on innocent commuters could instigate the downfall of an empire, but logic doesn't seem to be behind anything Aum Shinrikyo was involved in. Executed on a busy Monday morning, the attack killed 12 people and injured hundreds more. Remember this next time you're grumbling about your Monday morning commute.

If engaging in chemical warfare with ordinary, hardworking folk just riding the train to their desk jobs seems like a low thing to do, then you'd be right. But what do you expect from a group that also ordered the assassination of political cartoonist Yoshinori Kobayashi and allegedly kidnapped, murdered and incinerated the body of a cult member who dared to leave?

Sentenced to death by hanging in 2004, Shoko Asahara is currently still incarcerated after several appeals led to his execution date being postponed. Amazingly enough, the cult still operates under the name Aleph and, while it's had a clever change of branding, no one is fooled. As such, the group is under heavy surveillance by the Japanese authorities to ensure that no more humans (or sheep) are harmed in the name of whatever crap they use to justify murder.

You're now a member of ...

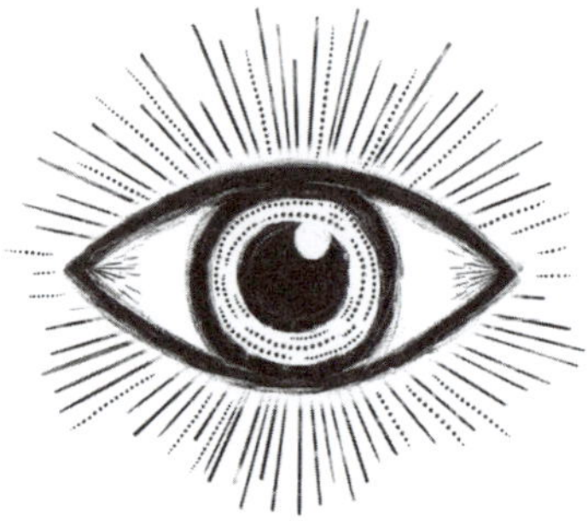

The Order of the Solar Temple

Ooh la la, you've just joined one of the most secretive (and affluent) cults in the world. Sadly, you've also joined one of the most deadly. As a member of the Order of the Solar Temple, you will follow a secret society-style sect, run from a headquarters located in Geneva, Switzerland. Drawn in by charismatic, cultured cult leaders, you'll probably enjoy life as a member of the Order of the Solar Temple, that is, unless you try to leave, and then you'll be deemed the Antichrist and be promptly murdered by other followers. But if you do choose to stay, you'll still face a pretty grim end. In the case of the Order of the Solar Temple, you're damned if you do and you're damned if you don't.

Formed in Geneva in 1984, the Order of the Solar Temple (OST) proves that there is much more to Switzerland than cheese, chocolate and meadows full of wild mushrooms. Old 'we're so neutral' Switzerland can harbour dangerous suicide-sects just like the rest of the world.

Started by Joseph Di Mambro and Luc Jouret, the Order of the Solar Temple merged many classic cult calling cards, including an end-of-the-world prophesy, a deep distrust of people not within the society, a good dash of magic and the occult, and murder of any members who try to leave.

Despite affluent members attending branches everywhere from Canada to Australia, the Order of the Solar Temple managed to keep most of its practices and beliefs secret, but what is known is that the group followed a New Age mix of Christianity combined with a little Freemasonry. While things seemed to go fine for the group for a little while, by the mid 90s, as is the case with so many cults, the leaders started to spiral out of control.

With Jouret becoming increasingly obsessed with sex, and many followers becoming sceptical of the questionable practices of their leaders, some members started speaking up for themselves. Big mistake. The cult leaders ordered the ritual murder of a follower (and his wife and infant child) who dared to publicly question their motives (although some claim that the murders took place because the baby had been identified as the Antichrist).

Believing that the end of the world was nigh, the cult leaders ordered the mass ritualistic suicide (or murder) of all cult members, in order for them to 'reach a higher plane' before the imminent destruction of the planet. Over the course of a few years, many mass suicide pacts were played out by cult members in Switzerland, France and Canada. Some members were asphyxiated, others shot, and some were drugged. Overall, 74 deaths have been attributed to the cult, making it one of the deadliest in the world, while simultaneously proving that wealthy people can fall victim to cults, too.

In general, religions tend to be exclusionary.

Women can't be priests, gay people aren't welcome at the Sunday service, unmarried mothers will be turned away at the Pearly Gates, and anyone with different beliefs is considered to be worshipping false idols.

Do you feel that mainstream religions should get on board with the whole multi-faith thing?

Yes! There is always room for believers of all kinds.

Find your cult on page 110

No. Mixing believers from different faiths is a recipe for trouble.

Turn to page 118 to keep searching

You're now a member of ...

The Raelian Movement

You've just joined a cult created by a retired French race car driver and journalist, famous for its belief in everything from UFOs to the rights of women to walk around topless. As a Raelian, you will spend your time swanning around in white robes (sometimes adorned with an oversized medallion necklace, if you're feeling in a ceremonial mood). Your days will most likely be spent protesting for women's rights (yes!), having lots of sex (yes!) and lobbying the government about the lack of cloning activity happening in the country (nope). Two out of three ain't bad.

Begun in 1974 by a Frenchman named Claude Vorilhon (who changed his name to Rael after a fateful encounter with an extraterrestrial being), the Raelian Movement is often referred to as 'that weird space sex cult'. Among many other things, Raelians believe that Jesus and Buddha were in fact aliens disguised as humans, who were sent to earth to spread messages of peace and love. They also believe in sexual freedom, with members encouraged to explore their sexuality and express themselves sexually with each other in a safe, consensual way. But there's much more to the Raelians than free love and aliens – there's also cloning, too!

Claiming to have produced the world's first human clone back in 2002, the Raelian Movement has also invested a lot of time in attempting to build an 'interplanetary embassy' in a number of countries, including Israel and Lebanon. To date, the embassy still hasn't been built, mainly because most governments seem to be a little wary of housing an embassy intended to welcome beings from outer space (did we not learn anything from watching *Independence Day*?) Having a logo that is essentially a hybrid of a swastika and the Star of David surely isn't helping their case either.

Ahead of their time, long before #freethenipple was a thing, the Raelian people were well into advocating for the rights of women to walk around topless. In fact, the Raelian people are the masterminds behind the Go Topless organisation – a group committed to equal topless rights for all (testify!).

Considering all of the above, do we really care if these people believe we are all descended from an alien race called the Elohim? By all accounts, the Raelians are supportive and welcoming of people of all genders, sexualities and races, and haven't started any world wars in the name of Rael. On one hand, Raelism makes total sense. On the other hand, it's batshit insane. Somewhere in between you'll probably find salvation. Until then, go forth and continue freeing the nipple dear Raelians (but please stop cloning people – it's creeping everyone out).

You're now a member of ...

Twelve Tribes

Roll up, roll up, you've just joined a cult started by a carnival worker! Now, just because Twelve Tribes was founded by a carnie, don't expect to be having any fun – this cult is one big, deceptive, money-making hall of mirrors. After being lured in by the promise of living in a community that eschews mainstream religion (in favour of their own brand of worship that sits somewhere between Christianity and Judaism), your time in Twelve Tribes will be spent working ridiculously long hours without pay. If that doesn't sound enticing enough, every aspect of your life will be governed by your spiritual leaders – from what you eat, to who you marry and what you read. Gulp.

Founded by an ex-carnival worker called Eugene Spriggs, Twelve Tribes started in Tennessee back in the 1960s and now has thousands of members living in communes all over the world. With communities located everywhere from England to Germany and beyond, Twelve Tribes emulates the Twelve Tribes of Israel in a curious mash-up of Christianity and Judaism, followed by a chaser of mind control.

Life is pretty strict within Twelve Tribes communities, so strict that almost everything you do is controlled by the rules of the tribe. Stimulants like coffee and tea are banned, as is sugar. Women are pretty much viewed as vessels for babies and are forbidden from choosing their own partner or using contraception. Forming ties with outsiders is discouraged and media consumption is banned, so there's little interaction with the outside world, with no televisions, newspapers or radios allowed within the community.

While all of this seems pretty grim, life appears to be particularly tough for children within Twelve Tribes. All children are home schooled and banned from playing with toys or reading fantasy novels. If you're having trouble imagining what your childhood would have been like without Harry Potter, Playstation or My Little Pony, spare a thought for the children of Twelve Tribes, who are also subjected to regular beatings for 'bad' behaviour. Despite being investigated for child abuse on many occasions, the Twelve Tribes communities stick by their commitment to corporal punishment.

So, what do you do all day if you're not going to school, aren't allowed to read a magazine, have no access to the Pirate Bay and can't even enjoy a cup of coffee? You work. And work and work and work. The women cook, clean and look after their many kids; the men do hard labour in fields, farms and on building sites. And none of them get paid.

Having discovered the secret to business success (i.e. using slave labour), Twelve Tribes run many profitable enterprises all over the world. From bakeries to construction businesses, Twelve Tribes may have eschewed things like modern medicine and the media, but golly have they embraced capitalism. It's unbelievable the profits you can make when you aren't paying your workers a dime to work 12–15-hour shifts.

Cults attract followers from all spectrums of society.

From the shy to the boisterous, wealthy to impoverished, the university-educated to people who never attended a day of school in their life, men and women, young and old.

In many ways, belonging to a cult is a great equaliser, with cults popping up on every continent except Antarctica (although it's arguable that a polar research station is the ultimate place to set up a cult, as there's nowhere to run when you want to leave).

Regardless of all the above, you've proven difficult to pin down. You're neither here nor there when it comes to interests and beliefs. You've flatly refused to take the cult bait and you just won't be categorised by a set of inane quiz questions and outlandish hypotheticals.

Are you ready?

Turn to page 86 to find out your spiritual fate, clever one.

You're now a member of ...

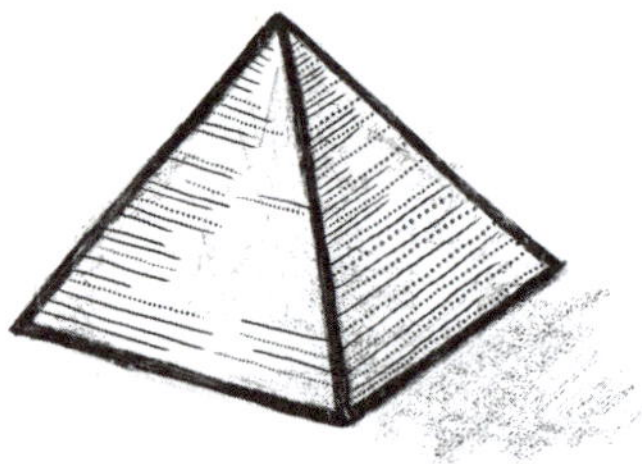

The Nuwaubian Nation

Get ready to walk like an Egyptian, you've just joined a black supremacist cult with an Ancient Egypt obsession that switched sides from Islam to UFO worship sometime in the late 80s. Gotta hand it to you, you've really joined a doozy of cult. As a member of the Nuwaubian Nation of Moors you will don Ancient Egyptian-style garb and follow the teachings and preachings of Malachi York – a musician, writer, conspiracy theorist and all-round super shady character. Originally based in New York and then Georgia, you may enjoy following Malachi York... until you find out who he really is (or isn't).

Malachi York (also known as Dwight York, Issa Al Haadi Al Mahdi and countless other pseudonyms) rose to prominence in Brooklyn, New York in the 1960s, around the same time that the Black Power movement was in full swing. With masses of people starting to move against the white patriarchy, Malachi York saw an opening to provide spiritual advice and promote black pride to the people of New York and beyond. Considering the state of civil rights in America in the 1960s, it's no surprise that he didn't have a hard time finding an audience.

Over the decades, York's ministry took many twists and turns, initially following Islam, then switching to more esoteric beliefs involving aliens and ancients. With York and his followers believing that modern day black people are indeed the master race, descended from Ancient Egyptians by way of aliens, York's message began to spread wide and far.

In between his spiritual duties, York wrote hundreds of books explaining his theories, formed a record label called Passion Productions and released a single called 'Only a Dream'. Reported to have run several money-making rackets in Brooklyn, no one could accuse York of being lazy – he was definitely one industrious cult leader.

York moved the Nuwaubian Nation headquarters from the streets of Brooklyn to rural Georgia in 1993 (apparently to avoid increasing scrutiny from the authorities). The new compound was a spectacular Ancient Egyptian-inspired complex of Vegas-style buildings including giant pyramids and a Sphinx (way to fly under the radar, York).

Of course, moving to avoid the authorities didn't do much. Following an investigation, Malachi York was found guilty of several counts of child abuse and racketeering, and was sentenced to a whopping 135 years in prison. Ever the conspiracy theorist, Malachi York and his supporters still claim that he was set up by the authorities and is innocent of all crimes. Despite their leader being incarcerated for horrific crimes, many people still follow the Nuwaubian Nation, such is the love and admiration for York and his teachings. Although the compound has been seized, sold and bulldozed, several Nuwaubian Nation bookstores still stand and a website riffing on York's innocence exists. While so many other cults originating from the 60s have disappeared, there's no keeping this cult down!

You're now a member of ...

The Church of God with Signs Following

'Praise the Lord!' I Hope you're not afraid of snakes, because you've just joined an American sect well into snake-handling and poison-drinking. As a member of the Church of God with Signs Following you'll be worshipping in a small, ramshackle church in the backwoods of a state such as Alabama, Tennessee or West Virginia (you better change your name to Cletus to fit in). At your church you'll listen to an evangelical preacher bang on about satanic forces, you will allow highly venomous snakes to crawl all over your body and you'll get stuck into a long cool drink of refreshing strychnine. As a part of this sect, your days are certainly numbered. If the cobras don't get you, at some stage the strychnine chaser will. But don't worry, it's God's Will.

Essentially, the Church of God with Signs Following is a collection of churches found all over North America (but especially in the Appalachian Mountains) that take the following Bible passage a little too literally:

> 'And these signs shall follow them that believe; In my name shall they cast out devils; they shall speak with new tongues; They shall take up serpents; and if they drink any deadly thing, it shall not hurt them; they shall lay hands on the sick, and they shall recover ...' – Mark 16:17-18

With services involving singing and praying with a side order of speaking in tongues, churchgoers also often play a few, fun rounds of pass-the-copperhead to show their mastery over demonic forces. If that's not enough some members of the congregation take things a little further and swallow poison in an attempt to prove the strength of their faith to protect them from forces of evil.

While handling snakes in churches has now been made illegal in many states of the USA, in the time since folk religions started snake-handling more than a hundred years ago, there have been more than sixty reported deaths in America from bites sustained during religious worship. Despite this, the authorities seem to mostly leave members of the Church of God with Signs Following alone, no doubt leaving them free to keep on competing in the Darwin Awards in the hope the sect will ultimately wipe themselves out through a process of natural selection.

FAQs

Are you a qualified cult specialist?

No. This book is the product of a misspent youth reading about Charles Manson, watching documentaries about the Jonestown massacre and watching the Waco siege play out on prime-time TV. Some kids play with Barbie dolls, others research cults.

Are all of the cults listed in this book really cults?

As you flip through this book, you will find 'cults' that are registered religions, retail organisations or pop culture jokes that got a little out of hand. For this reason, you should take everything within this book with a grain of salt.

How do I know if I'm in a cult?

In the words of Stephen Colbert, 'Here's an easy way to figure out if you're in a cult: If you're wondering whether you're in a cult, the answer is yes.'

How do I get help if I'm in a cult and want to get out?

This is really important. No one willingly joins a cult. People join communities that appear to provide solace, yet slowly suck the life out of those who fall into their clutches. The power that cult leaders have over their followers is astounding, yet often not surprising, given the brainwashing tactics commonly used to control and deceive unsuspecting people.

If you think you're in a cult and want to get out, here are some resources that may help you:

Holding Out HELP
holdingouthelp.org

Cult Education Institute
culteducation.com

Cult Watch
www.cultwatch.com

Recommended Reading

Shocked by what you've just read? Want to learn more about some of the cults in this book? Here's some utterly engrossing books on the subject (be prepared to be kept up until 3 am reading these babies in bed).

Amway: The Cult of Free Enterprise
Stephen Butterfield

Cults Inside Out: How People Get In and Can Get Out
Rick Alan Ross

Going Clear: Scientology, Hollywood, and the Prison of Belief
Lawrence Wright

Heaven's Gate: America's UFO Religion
Benjamin E. Zeller

Helter Skelter: The True Story of the Manson Murders
Vincent Bugliosi and Curt Gentry

Manson: The Life and Times of Charles Manson
Jeff Guinn

Prophet's Prey: My Seven-Year Investigation into Warren Jeffs and the Fundamentalist Church of Latter-Day Saints
Sam Brower

Raven: The Untold Story of the Rev. Jim Jones and His People
Tim Reiterman

Seductive Poison: A Jonestown Survivor's Story of Life and Death in the People's Temple
Deborah Layton

Stories from Jonestown
Leigh Fondakowski

The Abide Guide: Living Like Lebowski
Oliver Benjamin and Dwayne Eutsey

Troublemaker: Surviving Hollywood and Scientology
Leah Remini

The Source: The Untold Story of Father Yod, Ya Ho Wa 13, and The Source Family
Isis Aquarian, Erik Davis and Electricity Aquarian

Acknowledgements & About the Author

Acknowledgements

Writing a book is very much a team effort and there are many people who helped to get this book out of my brain and into your life. Many thanks to publishing genius Paul McNally from Smith Street Books for making this book happen and trusting me to do my thing. Huge kudos to Hannah Koelmeyer for being such a kickass editor and all-round excellent person. Special thanks to Stephanie Spartels whose clever design concept and illustrations make this book look better than I could ever have imagined and Heather Menzies for her nifty work with the layout. Thanks to everyone who suggested cults to include within the book – you sent me down many internet rabbit holes. Cheers to Kieron Sims for enduring a harrowing drive to Waco, Texas.

Cornball alert: While I'd like to thank everyone who ever encouraged or championed my writing, one person in particular played a pivotal role in my trajectory. My high school English teacher Anne Beams put me on the right path just in the nick of time, and without her guidance, tough love and genuine interest in my life, I wouldn't be a writer. Anne Beams is no longer with us, but she is the reason public education should be cherished and generously funded. Every high school student deserves an Anne Beams – regardless of their parent's income.

About the Author

Jo Stewart is a Melbourne-based writer whose words and images have been published in *The Sydney Morning Herald, The Age, The Saturday Paper, VICE, yen, Vacations & Travel* and *International Traveller*. From sailing to Antarctica in a yacht, to walking the dunes of the Simpson Desert with a caravan of camels, Jo has worked on expeditions to some of the world's most isolated, unforgiving places, including working on the *Shackleton: Death or Glory* documentary project that screened worldwide on Discovery Channel, SBS and PBS. Born with an eye for the absurd, Jo's teenage years were spent reading about cults, conspiracy theories and unsolved mysteries ... and nothing much has changed in adulthood.

Find out more at jostewart.com.au.

Smith Street Books

Published in 2017 by Smith Street Books
Melbourne | Australia
smithstreetbooks.com

ISBN: 978-1-925418-35-4

CIP data is available from the National Library of Australia.

Publisher: Paul McNally
Project editor: Hannah Koelmeyer, Tusk studio
Design concept and illustrations: Stephanie Spartels
Design layout: Heather Menzies, Studio31 Graphics

Printed & bound in China by C&C Offset Printing Co., Ltd.

Book 32
10 9 8 7 6 5 4 3 2 1